Photo by Rob Odorisio

A scene from the Manhattan Class Company production of "Five Women Wearing the Same Dress." Set design by Rob Odorisio.

FIVE WOMEN WEARING THE SAME DRESS

BY ALAN BALL

★

DRAMATISTS
PLAY SERVICE
INC.

FIVE WOMEN WEARING THE SAME DRESS
Copyright © 1993, Alan Ball

All Rights Reserved

SPECIAL NOTE

FIVE WOMEN WEARING THE SAME DRESS was first produced by Manhattan Class Company (Robert LuPone and Bernard Telsey, Executive Directors, W. D. Cantler, Associate Director), in New York City, on February 13, 1993. It was directed by Melia Bensussen; the set design was by Rob Odorisio; the lighting design was by Howard Werner; the costume design was by Karen Perry; the sound design was by Bruce Ellman, the production managers were Laura Kravets Gautier and Ira Mont, and the stage managers were Hazel Youngs and Katherine Lumb. The cast was as follows:

FRANCES	Dina Spybey
MEREDITH	Amelia Campbell
TRISHA	Ally Walker
GEORGEANNE	Betsy Aidem
MINDY	Allison Janney
TRIPP	Thomas Gibson

Understudies: Orlagh Cassidy, Jack Gwaltney and Linda Marie Larson.

CHARACTERS

FRANCES, a bridesmaid
MEREDITH, a bridesmaid
TRISHA, a bridesmaid
GEORGEANNE, a bridesmaid
MINDY, a bridesmaid
TRIPP, an usher

FIVE WOMEN
WEARING THE SAME DRESS

ACT ONE

The play takes place in Meredith's bedroom, a large, comfortable room on the second floor of a renovated turn-of-the-century mansion in a stylish, old-money suburb of Knoxville, Tennessee. There is a big brass bed, two large dressers, a vanity with a mirror. A compact shelf stereo system with CD player. A portable stair-climbing exercise machine. A large walk-in closet. A door leads to a bathroom; another to the hall. A large window with a window seat is suggested downstage.

The room has been decorated by Meredith's mother in a cluttered, eclectic combination of light Victorian and contemporary, mixing antiques and rich, deeply-hued linens & wallpaper with stark white custom shelving and high-tech lighting. A plush Persian rug covers the hardwood floor. Pillows abound. The effect is tasteful and inviting, not quite luxurious but definitely comfortable — it is clear this home is inhabited by the wealthy. The air of traditional privilege is disrupted, however, by a prominent poster of Malcolm X on the wall.

Underscoring the entire scene is an atmosphere of age and durability, conveyed by the original architectural details that remain: huge, multi-paned windows, exquisite molding, the sheer height of the ceiling. There is history in this room.

It is shortly after noon on a day in summer.

A few moments of silence, then someone knocks softly at the door.

FRANCES. *(Off.)* Yoo-hoo. *(After a moment the knock is repeated, slightly louder. Off.)* Anybody home? *(A long pause, then the door opens slowly and Frances peers around it.)* Meredith? *(Frances is a sweet-faced woman, twenty-one years old. She wears an expensive, off-the-shoulder bridesmaid's gown with a voluminous skirt, in peach or lilac or one of those horrible wedding pastels. She also wears an elaborate hat that matches her dress and she carries a bouquet. She enters the room tentatively and shuts the door behind her, moving stiffly in her dress, as if it intimidates her, which it does. She spots a jewelry box on top of the vanity, crosses to it, opens it and inspects its contents.)* Oh, my. *(She pulls out a glittering rhinestone bracelet. Handling it carefully, almost reverently, she puts it on her wrist and fastens it. Holding out her arm, she admires the bracelet in the mirror, assuming a series of poses she considers to be glamorous.)*

MEREDITH. *(Off.)* Mother, I am just going upstairs — *(A telephone somewhere in the room begins to ring. Off.)* I am not answering that. *(Alarmed, Frances struggles with the bracelet, vainly attempting to unfasten it. Meredith can be heard stomping up the stairs. Off.)* No ma'am, I am not answering that. You will not get to me this way. *(As Meredith gets closer, Frances panics. Unable to unfasten the rhinestone bracelet, she looks around the room for a place to hide. She scurries under the bed just as Meredith throws open the door and enters. Meredith is twenty-two years old. Athletic. Under a black leather motorcycle jacket she wears a dress identical to the one Frances wears; she seems resentful of it. She is also wearing a similar hat and carrying a bouquet. She has a beat-up backpack slung over one shoulder and sports a pair of sinister-looking sunglasses. She slams the door behind her and locks it, stares at the still-ringing telephone, frowns and picks up the receiver.)* Mother, what? I am just dropping off my stuff. No ma'am, this room is off limits to you today. Mother. Bye-bye. Bye-*bye. (She hangs up the receiver, then kicks off a pair of pumps died to match her dress, throws the bouquet and the backpack on the bed and crosses directly to the vanity. She grabs the jewelry box and digs through it.)* Shit! *(She checks the surface of the vanity frantically.)* I can't *believe* this!

(She crosses to the bed, pulls up the bedspread and then gets down on her hands and knees and reaches under the bed. Crying out.) Who is that?

FRANCES.   *(From under bed.)* Oh, it's just me. *(Frances emerges sheepishly from under the bed, keeping the bracelet on her wrist hidden behind her back. Sweetly.)* Hi, there.

MEREDITH.   Frances, what the hell are you doing?

FRANCES.   Oh, well, there aren't too many people downstairs, and nobody I really know too well, aside from Mama and Daddy and Uncle Reece and Aunt Kitty, so ... I guess I'm just looking for a friendly face. *(A nervous laugh.)*

MEREDITH.   Under my bed?

FRANCES.   No, I — well, when I heard you coming in, I got scared, I realized I really shouldn't be here. I tried to hide from you, Meredith. I hope you can forgive me.

MEREDITH.   *(Staring at her.)* Well, sure. *(She pulls a milk crate from underneath the bed and digs through it.)*

FRANCES.   *(Struggles with the bracelet behind her back.)* It's just that this room is so beautiful. I remember whenever we came to visit when I was little, and Tracy still lived in here? You and her and all the other cousins would be having tea parties in her playhouse out back, but I would sneak up here and sit in the middle of this room and pretend it was mine. Of course, I just worshiped her. Tracy.

MEREDITH.   You and everybody else. Herself included.

FRANCES.   That's why I was so thrilled to be in her wedding. *(Meredith, unable to find what she was looking for in the milk crate, shoves it back under the bed and groans in frustration.)*

MEREDITH.   Where the hell *is* it?

FRANCES.   *(Nervously.)* What are you looking for?

MEREDITH.   I am trying to find a joint that I was saving for this reception —

FRANCES.   A joint?

MEREDITH.   I know I had one in my jewelry box, and if Tracy took it, that would be just like her.

FRANCES.   Oh, surely she wouldn't!

MEREDITH.   Oh, surely she *would*.

FRANCES.   *(Shocked.)* Take drugs? On her wedding day?

MEREDITH. Have you noticed how calm she is today? How *serene?* She has been a nervous wreck for weeks. She had to be high. *(Catches sight of herself in the mirror.)* Oh, lord. *(Takes off her hat.)* And then she has the gall to make us wear these horrible — *things* on our heads, so we all look like the flying *nun* —

FRANCES. I like this hat.

MEREDITH. Are you serious? Look at yourself in the mirror, Frances, you look ridiculous.

FRANCES. Well —

MEREDITH. You look like a lamp. At least you can wear this dress, though. Makes me look like a linebacker. *(Meredith observes herself critically in the mirror, frowns, and gets a pack of cigarettes out of her backpack.)* You want one?

FRANCES. No thanks. I don't smoke. I'm a Christian.

MEREDITH. *(Digging through her backpack.)* Of course, wouldn't you know it? Now I can't find any matches. *(She goes into the bathroom, where she can be heard continuing her search. Frances works frantically to get the bracelet off her wrist.)* I mean, okay. I can certainly understand why Tracy would want to be stoned today, just to get through this ordeal. But she could have at least asked. I mean, she just *took* it! Typical. *(Frances finally gets the bracelet unclasped and slips it back into the jewelry box, greatly relieved.)*

FRANCES. *(Has learned her lesson.)* Thou shalt not covet.

MEREDITH. *(In bathroom.)* And then all that stuff about obedience, everybody was acting so serious, I was like, Tracy? Obey Scott? She already runs that poor boy's life. I mean, what a joke! Tracy, the blushing bride. Excuse me while I barf. *(Cries out.)* Oh, my God!!

FRANCES. *(Startled.)* What? *(Meredith enters from the bathroom holding a joint in front of her, reverently.)*

MEREDITH. Look. It was in the medicine chest! We are in business now! *(She grabs an ashtray and sits on the bed. Whining.)* Shit, we still don't have any matches! *(There is knock at the door. Irritated.)* Mother, I told you my room is off limits!

TRISHA. *(Off.)* Meredith?

MEREDITH.   Trisha! *(She leaves the joint and ashtray on the bed, crosses to the door, unlocks and opens it. Standing outside is Trisha, a striking, glamorous woman in her early thirties. She is dressed exactly like Meredith and Frances, but unlike them, she wears her dress well and moves gracefully in it. She carries a stylish, oversized shoulder bag.)*

TRISHA.   *(Cheerfully.)* Hey, babe!

MEREDITH.   Do you have any matches?

TRISHA.   Uhm, I think I might have a lighter.

MEREDITH.   Thank God! You just saved my life. *(Meredith motions her in and rushes back to the bed. Trisha enters and shuts the door behind her.)*

TRISHA.   *(Friendly.)* I would have gotten here sooner but some creep with whom I apparently share some sort of history cornered me in the parking lot and chewed my ear to a bloody stump about how great it was to see me again, and could we get together soon, and so I said sure, did he have three hundred dollars, just to shut him up.

MEREDITH.   Trisha! You didn't! What did he say?

TRISHA.   He asked if I could wait for him to run to a cash machine, can you believe it? *(Friendly.)* Hey, Frances!

FRANCES.   Hi there.

TRISHA.   How are you doing?

FRANCES.   I'm fine. Thank you so much for asking. *(Trisha crosses to the vanity.)*

TRISHA.   Oh, Meredith, your mother said she wants you downstairs to greet the guests while she freshens up.

MEREDITH.   Please. That woman hasn't been fresh in thirty years. While she pops a couple of Xanax is more like it.

TRISHA.   I could use a couple of those myself.

MEREDITH.   Well, as soon as you get that lighter out, we're going to get stoned.

TRISHA.   Oh, boy. I haven't been stoned in ages. Promise you won't let me do anything stupid, okay?

MEREDITH.   You would never do anything stupid.

TRISHA.   *(A laugh.)* Are you kidding? I looked out at the congregation during the ceremony, it was like half the men I saw, I think I may have slept with. God, I dread this reception. Do you think anyone would notice if I left?

MEREDITH.   Yes, don't you dare leave me here alone.

TRISHA.   *(Looking at her reflection in the vanity mirror.)* God, would you look at me? I look terrible.

MEREDITH.   You look like a million bucks, as usual.

TRISHA.   I had to put about a gallon of white-out underneath my eyes this morning. *(She pulls a cosmetics bag from her purse, and begins to skillfully retouch her make-up. The other women watch her, slightly cowed by her natural authority; this is a woman who knows how to be beautiful.)* So Frances, did you enjoy the wedding?

FRANCES.   Yes, it was so beautiful.

MEREDITH.   It was ridiculous.

FRANCES.   Tracy's dress sure was something.

MEREDITH.   Yeah, it was a float.

TRISHA.   You've got to hand it her, though, she carried it off. I could never wear anything like that with a straight face.

MEREDITH.   She didn't wear it. It wore *her.* If she has any sense at all, she'll put it on a mannequin and just roll it around the reception and leave herself free to mingle.

TRISHA.   I shudder to think how much that thing cost.

MEREDITH.   Six.

TRISHA.   *(Turns to her.)* That's obscene.

FRANCES.   Six hundred dollars?

MEREDITH.   Six *thousand.*

TRISHA.   She talked me into designing her invitations for *free*, and then she made me go through *eight* revisions, and she spent six thousand dollars on her *dress?* That is totally obscene. Your poor father must be paying a *fortune* for this wedding.

MEREDITH.   Don't you know it. But Daddy put his foot down — for a *change* — and said no way was he spending six thousand bucks on something she was only going to wear once, so she had to buy it herself.

TRISHA.   Wow. I guess she makes pretty good money working for Pepsi.

MEREDITH.   I guess. She offered to get me an interview over there. I told her I would rather work at McDonald's. I have spent my entire life being Tracy Marlowe's little sister, the last thing I want to do is go work at the same place she does. Trisha! Where is that lighter?

TRISHA. *(Handing her purse to Meredith.)* It's in there somewhere.

MEREDITH. Good lord, what the hell do you keep in this thing?

TRISHA. Only my entire life. *(Meredith starts to dig through the purse.)*

MEREDITH. I about died when they knelt down and somebody had painted "Help Me" on the soles of Scott's shoes —

FRANCES. Oh, I *hated* that. How could somebody do something so nasty? A wedding is a sacred occasion.

MEREDITH. Well, *I* thought it was priceless.

TRISHA. Yeah, I figured you thought that was pretty funny.

MEREDITH. I wasn't the one who did it, if that's what you're implying. I wish I had been. Trisha! Do you know who did? Who? Tell me.

TRISHA. I don't know.

MEREDITH. You lie.

TRISHA. Meredith, I have no idea. It could be any one of those overgrown frat boys.

MEREDITH. I wish I knew which one. I would give him a blow job. *(She pulls an accordion-pack of condoms from Trisha's purse.)* God, do you think you have enough condoms here?

TRISHA. Hey, the scout motto is be prepared.

MEREDITH. That's the boy scout motto.

TRISHA. Well, then, the girl scout motto is be extra prepared, because chances are the boy scout is an irresponsible jerk. *(Meredith finds the lighter and lights the joint. She inhales deeply.)*

MEREDITH. *(Exhales, laughs.)* "Help me."

FRANCES. Pew! That stuff stinks.

TRISHA. Poor Scott. He turned about three shades of red, didn't he? I think he thought he had done something wrong.

MEREDITH. He did. He married my sister, that's about as wrong as you can get. God, I'm glad I found this joint.

TRISHA. I think Scott and Tracy are a perfect match.

11

FRANCES.   Oh, I do too.

TRISHA.   They're both smart, good-looking, rich —

MEREDITH.   *Really* white.

FRANCES.   And you can tell he really loves her.

MEREDITH.   Yeah, well, any dog loves its master.

TRISHA.   Now, Meredith, be nice.

MEREDITH.   Oh, Trisha, don't be such a cheerleader. I want to have fun today. Fat chance. Everybody here is so aggressively *normal*, it's like the bland leading the bland. I was hoping Scott's lesbian sister would perk things up, but she's about as much fun as having your teeth cleaned.

FRANCES.   *(Shocked.)* Scott's sister is a — a — and everybody just *knows* about it?

TRISHA.   I guess. *(To Meredith.)* She's pretty much out, isn't she?

MEREDITH.   God, yes. She rubs it in everybody's face.

FRANCES.   My goodness. I don't think I've ever seen one before.

MEREDITH.   Well, now you've seen three.

FRANCES.   Who else?

MEREDITH.   Those two flute players that played during the ceremony.

FRANCES.   You're kidding.

MEREDITH.   Nope.

FRANCES.   But — they looked just like *real* women. And them playing in church like that, isn't that kind of sacrilegious?

TRISHA.   I don't think you need to worry about it, Frances.

MEREDITH.   Really. So far, this has been the most candy-ass wedding I've ever been to in my life. Things better pick up at the reception. I want something really sick and fucked up to happen. *(Trisha, having finished touching up her makeup, crosses to Meredith and takes the joint from her.)*

TRISHA.   *(Laughs.)* To you or to someone else?

MEREDITH.   Either way, I don't give a shit.

TRISHA.   Well, I bet you won't be disappointed.

MEREDITH.   *(Senses dirt.)* Why? What's going on?

TRISHA.   Nothing.

12

MEREDITH.   Tell me.

TRISHA.   *(Offering joint to Frances.)* Frances, you want some of this?

FRANCES.   No ma'am. I do not take drugs. I'm a Christian.

TRISHA.   I'm so sorry.

MEREDITH.   It's Georgeanne, isn't it?

TRISHA.   What?

MEREDITH.   I saw her crying during the ceremony.

TRISHA.   So? Lots of people cry at weddings.

MEREDITH.   No, this had nothing to do with the wedding. *(Pause.)* Come on, Trisha, you have to tell me.

TRISHA.   Meredith, I don't know. Georgeanne and I are not all that close anymore.

MEREDITH.   *(Suddenly, surprised.)* It's Tommy Valentine, isn't it. It's because he's here today.

TRISHA.   I seriously doubt it.

FRANCES.   Tommy Valentine. I have been trying to think of his name all day.

MEREDITH.   Georgeanne had a thing with him too?

TRISHA.   About a hundred years ago.

MEREDITH.   *(A whine.)* My God, is there *anybody* who didn't do it with him? *(Pause.)* I guess when you're as good looking as he is ...

TRISHA.   He's not *that* good looking.

MEREDITH.   Trisha. He is sweat-out-loud gorgeous. That man is walking sex. Why else would every single one of you go off the deep end over him?

TRISHA.   I never went off the deep end over him.

MEREDITH.   Right.

TRISHA.   I didn't.

FRANCES.   I met him once, when Tracy brought him to that family reunion at Uncle Reece and Aunt Kitty's lake house? He was real nice.

MEREDITH.   *(To Trisha.)* You look me in the eye and tell me you did not have a thing with him.

TRISHA.   I did not have a thing with him.

MEREDITH.   Trisha.

TRISHA.   We went out a few times, before he and Tracy

13

ever got together. As a matter of fact, I introduced them to each other.

MEREDITH.   I know.

TRISHA.   So how do you know everything? You were only a little kid.

MEREDITH.   I was a smart little kid. And I also happen to be sisters with Tracy the mouth.

TRISHA.   Well, then you probably know more than I do.

MEREDITH.   I didn't know about Georgeanne and Tommy Valentine. *(Georgeanne enters. In her early thirties, she wears the same dress and hat as the others and carries an opened bottle of champagne. Her hat is slightly askew. She bursts through the door, slams it behind her, kicks it once and then leans against it, crying, unaware there is anyone else in the room.)*

GEORGEANNE.   *(Kicking the door again.)* You stupid fucker! *(She wipes her nose on part of her dress and takes a swig from the champagne bottle, then turns and sees the others. An awkward pause.)* Well, hello there.

TRISHA.   Hey, hon.

MEREDITH.   *(Sweetly.)* Hey, Georgeanne.

GEORGEANNE.   Please excuse me. *(She goes into the bathroom and slams the door.)*

MEREDITH.   *(Thrilled.)* Whoa. *(Trisha crosses to the window and looks out.)*

TRISHA.   They sure are taking their sweet time setting up that bar. Man, I love a good open bar. If I ever get to heaven and there's not an open bar, God is going to have some serious explaining to do to me.

FRANCES.   There will most certainly *not* be any liquor in heaven.

TRISHA.   Well, thank you for clarifying that for me, Frances. I'll be sure to bring my own.

MEREDITH.   *(Whispering.)* Tommy must have said something to Georgeanne to get her that upset, don't you think?

TRISHA.   Meredith, why do you even care?

MEREDITH.   Maybe it's her husband! I notice he's not here today, I bet he's cheating on her!

TRISHA.   Jesus.

MEREDITH. *(Gleefully.)* I bet he's cheating on her and she just found out! You think?

TRISHA. I think it's none of your fucking business. Her life is her life, it's not a source of personal entertainment for you. That's pathetic.

MEREDITH. *(Stung.)* I'm sorry. God.

TRISHA. I suppose you've never been through anything you didn't want the whole world to watch?

MEREDITH. I said I was sorry. You don't have to bite my head off. *(Pause.)*

TRISHA. Well. I'm just a little sensitive about that particular issue, since I am the reigning queen of the bad rep.

MEREDITH. *(Not quite heartfelt.)* Your reputation is fine.

TRISHA. You shouldn't lie, Meredith, if you can't do it any better than that.

MEREDITH. I have never heard anybody say one bad thing about you.

TRISHA. Your mother used to habitually refer to me as "that little whore."

MEREDITH. You're crazy. Mama always loved you.

TRISHA. Meredith. Your mother hated my guts. She still does. She will not look me in the eye to this day.

MEREDITH. Why would she hate you?

TRISHA. Because she thought I was the world's worst influence on Tracy. And I was. But it is just basic human nature to be a real degenerate every now and then. And you ought to be able to do it without the whole world looking down its nose at you and acting like it's anything out of the ordinary. *(Looking out window.)* Oh, God. There's the earring.

MEREDITH. *(Joins her at window.)* What?

TRISHA. That cute-boy usher, with the earring.

MEREDITH. Oh, him. He's Scott's cousin.

TRISHA. He is a piece of work.

MEREDITH. Ugh, you think?

TRISHA. Uh-huh.

FRANCES. *(Brightly.)* You know, my big sister was dating a boy who had an earring, but Mama and Daddy made her break up with him.

MEREDITH.   Frances, your sister is two years older than *me.*
FRANCES.   Is she?
MEREDITH.   And she still lets her parents tell her what to do? That is fucked.
FRANCES.   *(Flushed.)* Meredith, the Bible says to honor thy Father and Mother.
MEREDITH.   The Bible also says that eating shellfish is an abomination, but that didn't stop you from sucking down that lobster bisque at the rehearsal dinner.
TRISHA.   What is his name?
MEREDITH.   His name is Tripp Davenport and you know it. *(Trisha looks at her.)* Oh come on, he flirted with you all through the rehearsal dinner.
TRISHA.   Yeah, but he never told me his name.
MEREDITH.   Well, his real name is Griffin Lyle Davenport the Third.
TRISHA.   I think Tripp suits him better. He's got that look, you know?
MEREDITH.   What look?
TRISHA.   That look that makes you feel like you're at a really boring party and you and he are the only ones with drugs. It's the same look Tommy Valentine has.
MEREDITH.   You'll have to point it out to me.
TRISHA.   Oh, no. Believe me, you would be better off if you never even saw that look. It always turns out to be more trouble than it is worth.
MEREDITH.   Look at all of them, in their tuxes. They look like a bunch of big — birds, you know?
TRISHA.   Pigeons. *(Laughs.)* They are *pumped.*
MEREDITH.   Why are men so stupid?
TRISHA.   Because they're allowed to be.
MEREDITH.   They are so weird. They are so weird.
TRISHA.   Which one do you want?
MEREDITH.   The only one of them that doesn't totally gross me out is Frank.
TRISHA.   Frank? Really?
MEREDITH.   I still remember what he was wearing the time he came to pick up Tracy for the Valentine's Dance when

16

they were in eighth grade. A white leisure suit with blue stripes, a navy blue shirt and a white tie. A white belt and white shoes with big silver buckles. I thought he was the most gorgeous thing I had ever seen.

TRISHA. He is handsome.

MEREDITH. He's a fag, isn't he.

TRISHA. Well —

MEREDITH. I knew it. What a waste.

TRISHA. Meredith, that is a terrible thing to say.

MEREDITH. I meant it as a compliment.

TRISHA. Calling somebody a waste is not a compliment. *(Pause.)*

FRANCES. Billy.

TRISHA. What?

FRANCES. He's the one I want.

TRISHA. Scott's little brother?

MEREDITH. Frances, he's fifteen.

FRANCES. I know.

TRISHA. Frances, you are *bad.* You're a wild woman, aren't you? *(Georgeanne enters from the bathroom.)*

GEORGEANNE. Yo.

MEREDITH. Hey, Georgeanne.

TRISHA. Hey, babe. You okay?

GEORGEANNE. No, I'm all fucked up. *(She sits on the edge of the bed, stares at the others and starts to cry. Pause.)*

MEREDITH. *(Nosy.)* What's wrong, Georgeanne? You can tell us. We won't tell anybody, I swear.

TRISHA. Meredith.

MEREDITH. It might do you some good to talk about it.

TRISHA. Meredith, why don't you and Frances go see if they've set up that bar yet?

MEREDITH. Why don't you just look out the window? *(Trisha makes a "just get out of here" face at Meredith, who makes a "why can't I stay" face back at her.)* Oh, all right. Y'all are going to have to wait for me to put on another pair of shoes, though. I am not wearing those peach-colored Chinese torture devices one minute longer. *(She goes into her closet. An awkward moment.)*

GEORGEANNE.   Hey, Frances.

FRANCES.   Hi there.

GEORGEANNE.   Look. I know we don't know each other at all, but I am sorry you have to see me like this.

FRANCES.   It's okay. Jesus wept. *(Meredith emerges from the closet carrying a pair of men's athletic shoes, sits on the bed and puts them on.)*

GEORGEANNE.   One of those bartenders, the bald-headed one? If you flirt with him, he'll give you a bottle of champagne.

MEREDITH.   I can't do that.

FRANCES.   I can. You'll have to drink the champagne, though, because —

MEREDITH.   You're a Christian. I know. How do I look? *(Checks herself in the mirror.)* Hideous.

TRISHA.   You look fine.

MEREDITH.   Yeah, right. *(Grabs Frances.)* Come on, Frances.

FRANCES.   *(Sweetly.)* Bye-bye now!

MEREDITH.   *(Mimicking Frances.)* Bye-bye, now! *(Meredith and Frances exit. Trisha shuts the door behind them but remains standing.)*

TRISHA.   Please do not tell me this is about Tommy Valentine. *(Georgeanne nods, ashamed.)*

GEORGEANNE.   I was walking down the aisle, first thing I saw was the back of his head. It just jumped right out at me. I recognized that little hair pattern on the back of his neck, where his hair starts? You know where it comes to those two little points, and it's darker than the rest? I always thought that was so sexy. Then I looked at him during the ceremony, and something about the way the light hit his face ... I swear, it just broke my heart. And then outside, I saw him talking to this total bitch in a navy blue linen dress with absolutely no back, I mean you could almost see her butt. And he was smiling at her with that smile, that same smile that used to make me feel like I really meant something to him. And then it all came back, just bang, all those times I sat waiting for his phone call, me going out of my way to make things convenient for him. Having to take a fucking taxi cab to the

Women's Health Center that day because it was so cold my car wouldn't start. And later that awful, awful night I sat out in front of his apartment building staring at Tracy's burgundy Cutlass in the driveway, just wishing I was dead. You know, I started smoking cigarettes that night. And if I ever die of cancer I swear it's going to be Tommy Valentine's fault. *(She lights a cigarette, stands and wanders around listlessly.)* God! I feel like I am going crazy! My cousin George, he's a nurse, he says I am the perfect type to get some weird disease because I'm so emotional.

TRISHA. You're not going crazy. You're just being really dramatic and self-indulgent.

GEORGEANNE. Self-indulgent! You think I want to feel like this?

TRISHA. Nobody's making you. *(Pause. Georgeanne stares at her, then takes a swig from the champagne bottle.)*

GEORGEANNE. All right. Enough about me, more about my *dress*. Can you believe Tracy made us wear these things?

TRISHA. Yes.

GEORGEANNE. Of course, I can't believe she asked me to be in her wedding —

TRISHA. I can't believe you accepted.

GEORGEANNE. Well, I didn't have any choice, Trisha. What was I supposed to say? Tracy, I don't think I can be in your wedding, because you remember when I had that nervous breakdown my junior year of college? That was because your boyfriend knocked me up and I had to have an abortion all by myself while he was taking you to the Kappa Sig Luau, and things have been just a little, well, *strained* between you and me ever since.

TRISHA. Have you ever talked to her about that?

GEORGEANNE. Oh. No, neither one of us has ever mentioned it. *(Looking out window.)* And now here she is, getting married to Scott McClure, the biggest piece of wet toast I ever saw in my life. 'Course I married Chuck Darby, the *second* biggest piece of wet toast I ever saw, because I thought I wanted some *stability*. And there's Tommy Valentine, getting ready to rip that little bitch's backless linen dress off of her scrawny little body and fuck her brains out. God, I wish I was her.

TRISHA. *(Exasperated.)* Oh, please. You do not.

GEORGEANNE. Oh, yes I do. I am wearing over a hundred dollars worth of extremely uncomfortable lingerie from Victoria's Secret that I bought specifically for him to rip off of *me.*

TRISHA. *(Staring at her.)* You honestly thought you were going to sleep with Tommy Valentine today?

GEORGEANNE. Well. Yeah, I mean, why not? Remember page 67 of *The Godfather?*

TRISHA. I think your memories of him might be just a little rosy, I mean it has been almost, what, ten years?

GEORGEANNE. Three months.

TRISHA. Excuse me? *(Georgeanne nods guiltily.)* Georgeanne, you better spill your guts to me right now.

GEORGEANNE. I ran into him at this sleazy bar that only plays fifties and sixties music? I hate those places but at least I'm not the oldest one there. He seemed really happy to see me, and then we started flirting, but it wasn't gross, it was real sweet — *(Trisha laughs.)* I'm serious, it was.

TRISHA. I'm so sure.

GEORGEANNE. You weren't there!

TRISHA. I've been there. So then what happened?

GEORGEANNE. Well, we closed that bar, and he asked me if I wanted to go somewhere where we could be alone. I said, look, this is not a good idea, I'm married, I have a little boy. And once I said that? It's like I didn't have to worry about it. I had said it, so it was out of the way. And I just went nuts, we ended up doing it in the parking lot, on the concrete, right behind a Dempsey Dumpster. *(Pause.)*

TRISHA. *(Impressed.)* Wow. That's pretty good.

GEORGEANNE. Trisha, it was the best sex I ever had in my entire life. I will never, ever be able to smell garbage again without thinking about it. So my memories of Tommy are pretty recent and pretty accurate, I think.

TRISHA. Yeah, but Georgeanne. Did he call you after that?

GEORGEANNE. No.

TRISHA. Okay, so here's this guy who totally bagged out on

his responsibility to you, left you to go through an abortion all by yourself. Ten years later, he fucks you in a parking lot and then he ignores you. And you still want him.

GEORGEANNE.   I can't help it. I love him.

TRISHA.   That's not love, that's addiction.

GEORGEANNE.   Well, I'm sorry, but I hadn't had sex in over a year. And I wouldn't mind making a habit of it.

TRISHA.   What? *(Pause.)*

GEORGEANNE.   Chuck and I don't even sleep in the same bed anymore. He sleeps in the guest room.

TRISHA.   Why?

GEORGEANNE.   I don't know.

TRISHA.   You have some idea. You have to.

GEORGEANNE.   He doesn't talk to me, Trisha. It's like I'm not even there. I told Chuck about Tommy, the next day. He just looked at me with this fish face, and then he said, "You don't have to tell me everything you do." *(She starts to cry.)*

TRISHA.   *(Irritated.)* Georgeanne!

GEORGEANNE.   What can I do?

TRISHA.   *Make* Chuck talk to you. Make him go to a counselor.

GEORGEANNE.   No.

TRISHA.   Do you want to save your marriage?

GEORGEANNE.   No! I *don't!* I never should have married him in the first place, just like you said. I don't love him. I don't even like him! *(Suddenly, the door opens and Mindy enters. She is an attractive, slender woman in her mid-to-late-thirties. She is dressed exactly like the others.)*

MINDY.   Y'all, am I bleeding?

TRISHA.   Not that I can see.

MINDY.   *(Goes to mirror.)* Well, I will be. I am having one of those days where I just can't stop running into things? Do you ever have those? I am usually a very graceful woman, but something about this dress, it makes me feel like Bigfoot. I just ran smack dab into a cabinet in the kitchen, just walked right straight into it. Like there was a big magnet in that cabinet and I had a steel plate in my head. Ka-BOOM. I will

21

probably need stitches by the time this reception is over. *(Turns to them.)* I am terrified. Terrified I am going to do something to ruin this wedding, and Scott will never forgive me. Just like that time I ralphed right in the middle of his Eagle Scout induction ceremony. My therapist thinks I was jealous that I couldn't be an eagle scout, but I don't think that was it. I mean, I was nineteen. I think I had just had a bad tuna salad sandwich. *(Notices Georgeanne's tears.)* Oh, this is a bad time, isn't it? I'm so sorry. I'll leave. *(She exits, knocking something over in the process.)* See what I mean? *(Pause.)*

GEORGEANNE.   Are they all like that?

TRISHA.   Who?

GEORGEANNE.   You know. Lesbians.

TRISHA.   What, clumsy?

GEORGEANNE.   She's just so, I don't know. Blunt. Are they all like that?

TRISHA.   Why are you asking me?

GEORGEANNE.   *(Evasively.)* Well, you know ...

TRISHA.   No, what?

GEORGEANNE.   Well, haven't ... I mean, I just remember hearing something about you and ... oh, forget it.

TRISHA.   *(Smiling.)* All the lesbians I have known have not been clumsy. As a matter of fact, Mindy is the first.

GEORGEANNE.   She is so strange.

TRISHA.   I like her.

GEORGEANNE.   Me, too, I guess. She seems to thoroughly detest Tracy, so she can't be all bad. *(Georgeanne crosses to the vanity. Looking in mirror.)* God. Look at me. I am totally pathetic. I just don't want to be alone. Is that too much to ask? I mean, I still believe in marriage. I do. *(Trisha laughs ruefully.)* You don't?

TRISHA.   To be perfectly honest with you, Georgeanne, I think any woman who chooses marriage in this day and age is out of her fucking mind.

GEORGEANNE.   Don't you believe in love?

TRISHA.   *(Turning to her.)* I certainly believe in consideration. And respect. And I definitely believe in sex, because it's healthy and necessary. But love, what is that? I have had so

22

many guys tell me they loved me, and not a single one of them has made any difference in my life.

GEORGEANNE.   Maybe you haven't met the right one.

TRISHA.   Oh, please. I've met him more times than I'd care to admit.

GEORGEANNE.   Well, maybe you just haven't given him a chance.

TRISHA.   I have given him too many chances.

GEORGEANNE.   Oh, come on. What's the longest relationship you ever had, how many hours did that last?

TRISHA.   Well, why drag it out? He'll just start trying to run my life or else he'll want me to be his mother.

GEORGEANNE.   Not all men are like that.

TRISHA.   I have yet to meet one who isn't. And I seriously doubt if I ever will.

GEORGEANNE.   Really?

TRISHA.   Yeah.

GEORGEANNE.   How can you live like that?

TRISHA.   (A laugh.) Well, in the first place, it's not a major tragedy, I'm just being honest. (Pause.)

GEORGEANNE.   Maybe you're right. I'm probably just a hopeless romantic, doomed to go through my life being disappointed. (At window.) There he goes. Sniffing after little Miss Navy Blue Linen. God. Look at the way he walks ... he sure can wear a pair of pants.

TRISHA.   I mean, what's the payoff? For having had that many women? Does it make him feel accomplished? Wiser? Or has it just become this drug he has to have?

GEORGEANNE.   Well, you've slept with just as many guys. What's the payoff for you?

TRISHA.   I have not slept with as many guys!

GEORGEANNE.   How many guys *have* you slept with?

TRISHA.   I don't know. A hundred.

GEORGEANNE.   A hundred!

TRISHA.   I haven't kept *count*.

GEORGEANNE.   Trisha! That's a lot.

TRISHA.   Yeah, but Tommy Valentine is like Wilt Chamberlain, he's probably had sex with a *thousand* women.

GEORGEANNE.   God, I wonder if he's ever had an AIDS test.

TRISHA.   You better hope so. Did he use a condom in the parking lot?

GEORGEANNE.   No.

TRISHA.   Georgeanne.

GEORGEANNE.   I know. *(Pause.)* You think he's ever done it with another man?

TRISHA.   A guy like Tommy, as good looking as he is? I'm sure he's had opportunities.

GEORGEANNE.   Yeah, but he's way too good in bed to be a queer.

TRISHA.   That doesn't mean a thing. I knew this lifeguard once, talk about good in bed, this boy could have taught old Tommy Valentine a trick or two. He was a total animal, he loved sex. Loved it. Then one day I showed up at his apartment and found him in bed with the telephone repairman, which is obviously why I hadn't been able to call to tell him I was on my way.

GEORGEANNE.   Oh my God. What did you do?

TRISHA.   I went to happy hour at Bennigan's and picked up a busboy. *(Pause.)*

GEORGEANNE.   Have *you* ever had an AIDS test?

TRISHA.   Yep.

GEORGEANNE.   I'm too scared to take it. I mean, I know the chances are slim, but with *my* luck. Weren't you scared?

TRISHA.   Yeah, I was.

GEORGEANNE.   What made you go through with it?

TRISHA.   Well, it seemed like the responsible thing to do, and ... that lifeguard died.

GEORGEANNE.   Shit, Trisha. He died of AIDS? *(Trisha nods.)* You're okay, aren't you?

TRISHA.   Yes, Georgeanne. I'm fine.

GEORGEANNE.   Oh my God. I never knew anybody who actually had it.

TRISHA.   You will. *(Pause.)*

GEORGEANNE.   Well, I certainly don't want Tommy Valentine to have AIDS. But I tell you one thing. I can't wait for him to lose his looks.

TRISHA.   And he will. It's bound to catch up with him. He's going to end up one of those hatchet-faced old men that really handsome guys turn into.

GEORGEANNE.   Yes. He'll have one of those big red Ted Kennedy noses from drinking so much his whole life.

TRISHA.   And a beer gut.

GEORGEANNE.   He'll lose his hair.

TRISHA.   He'll wear golf pants.

GEORGEANNE.   Green golf pants. That are too tight.

TRISHA.   Yes! And he'll unbutton his shirts a couple of buttons more than he should. *(Pause.)*

GEORGEANNE.   No. He won't do any of that. He'll just get better looking as he gets older, he'll never gain any weight, he'll wear a T-shirt and blue jeans and have grey hair and he will be so gorgeous that it hurts just to look at him. *I*, on the other hand, will be as big as a house, I'll wear too much makeup, I won't have any hair left from a lifetime of bad perms, and I'll get skin cancer from going to the lake too much when I was in high school and I'll just wake up one morning and I'll be dead. And Tommy Valentine will read my obituary in the paper and it won't even occur to him that he ever even knew me, much less slept with me. *(She bursts out laughing.)*

TRISHA.   You were right. You *are* crazy.

GEORGEANNE.   I am one sick ticket. Well, I guess I should give up my fantasy of getting laid by Sonny Corleone today.

TRISHA.   Not necessarily. There are lots of cute guys here.

GEORGEANNE.   Yeah, I dare you to find one who is straight, single and who has a job.

TRISHA.   Maybe you need to lower your expectations.

GEORGEANNE.   Maybe I need to have a nervous breakdown. Maybe I need to have a big, loud, nasty, smelly nervous breakdown right when Dr. Marlowe goes to do his father-of-the-bride dance with the new and improved Tracy Marlowe hyphen McClure.

TRISHA.   I'll give you twenty bucks if you do.

GEORGEANNE.   Do not tempt me, Trisha. I just might.

(Meredith bursts in.)

MEREDITH. I will give you a hundred bucks. I will give you anything you want. I will give you this pair of one-carat diamond studs I got for graduation.

TRISHA. Meredith!

MEREDITH. *(Rummaging through her jewelry box.)* I will give you this antique ring that belonged to my grandmother that has been appraised at over five hundred dollars. See that? Isn't it pretty? It's yours.

TRISHA. How long have you been standing out there?

MEREDITH. *(Innocently.)* I just heard that last little bit, I swear.

TRISHA. I cannot *believe* you.

MEREDITH. Please, Georgeanne, please say you will.

GEORGEANNE. No, Meredith. I will not.

MEREDITH. Please?

GEORGEANNE. *No.* I am *not* going to cause a scene.

MEREDITH. *(Whining.)* Why not?

GEORGEANNE. Because this is your sister's wedding day, and that would be a really rotten thing for me to do. I may be a bitch, and I may be a slut, but I do have some standards.

MEREDITH. Shit.

TRISHA. Why are you so intent on something happening today, Meredith?

MEREDITH. I just hate this whole thing. I hate it. It's so goddamn fake it makes me sick. *(She lights a cigarette and crosses to the window, irritated.)*

TRISHA. Where's Frances?

MEREDITH. She's down there sucking up to that baldheaded bartender and he is a complete geek, if you ask me. *(Trisha and Georgeanne join her at the window to watch.)*

TRISHA. Oh, he looks nice.

MEREDITH. Gross. His Adam's apple is as big as my head.

GEORGEANNE. At least he's not wearing a rug. I swear, sometimes I look at my husband and his toupee is sitting up on top of his head like a stale pancake, and my heart just goes out to him. I mean, does he think people don't *know?*

A ten-year-old *child* can tell. *(Mindy enters with a plate of finger foods.)*

MINDY.   I wish I had one of those lobster bibs, I just know I'm going to be wearing this food any minute now. Of course, it's not like I plan to ever wear this dress again.

MEREDITH.   *(Sarcastically.)* Sure you will. Have it taken up, wear it as a cocktail dress. It'll be sweet.

MINDY.   I'll probably give it to my friend Leroy, he's the only person I know who can wear this color. Anyway. Mrs. Marlowe sent me up here to tell y'all to come downstairs right this instant. She might have just wanted me out of her dining room, she was looking at me with this frozen smile, I could see every vein in her neck. Like, please God, just keep her away from my crystal. But she said for me to tell you all that it was a poor reflection on Tracy for all her bridesmaids to be avoiding the reception.

MEREDITH.   Oh, well, God forbid we should make Tracy look bad.

GEORGEANNE.   Why not, she's made every single one of us look perfectly dreadful.

MINDY.   I like this dress.

GEORGEANNE.   You do not.

MINDY.   I do. I am so glamorous in this dress, I am goddamn Leona Helmsley. I am the queen of my own empire with a heavily armed security force. I am woman, hear me fucking roar.

TRISHA.   Now do you think Tracy really thought these looked nice, or was it a conscious attempt to surround herself with ridiculous-looking women so that she would look better?

MEREDITH.   What do you think?

GEORGEANNE.   Like she needs to look better.

TRISHA.   She is one beautiful woman.

GEORGEANNE.   She is perfect. Perfect.

MEREDITH.   She always has been.

MINDY.   I hate her.

GEORGEANNE.   I have no idea who she is now.

MINDY.   I don't want to know.

GEORGEANNE.   I'm serious.

MEREDITH. She's a rich white Republican bitch.

GEORGEANNE. Meredith! She's your sister.

MEREDITH. So? Y'all are trashing her, too.

TRISHA. I used to know her. Really well, I thought.

GEORGEANNE. You guys were tight.

TRISHA. For a while. But it was one of those friendships, you know, that's based on giving each other permission to be just totally wild and irresponsible? Those never last.

GEORGEANNE. She is — in *Glamour* magazine, you know the do's and don't's? She is the ultimate "do" girl.

TRISHA. And we're all the "don't" girl.

MEREDITH. Not you, Trisha.

TRISHA. Please.

GEORGEANNE. Oh, please my butt. You're the only friend Tracy ever had who was pretty as she is. You're probably the first girl she ever met who wasn't intimidated by her.

MINDY. No wonder she liked you. What freedom.

TRISHA. We had a lot of fun. That's why it's so weird now. I can barely carry on a conversation with her. We have absolutely nothing in common.

MEREDITH. Except Tommy Valentine.

TRISHA. And we're members of quite a large club in that respect.

GEORGEANNE. Wait a minute. Don't you think this is kind of weird?

MINDY. What?

GEORGEANNE. That we're all in her wedding but not one of us is really her friend?

MEREDITH. She had to dig, too. Look at my dorky cousin Frances.

GEORGEANNE. Good lord. I grew up with Tracy, I was her ugly sidekick all throughout high school and college, but I haven't been close to her in years.

TRISHA. Me neither.

GEORGEANNE. Doesn't she have any real friends?

MINDY. Don't look at me. Tracy and I move in very different circles.

GEORGEANNE. Meredith?

MEREDITH.   I don't know. Seems like she hangs out with Mama an awful lot.

GEORGEANNE.   I don't believe it. Here she is, the perfect woman, the ultimate do girl. She's beautiful, she has a great body, she has a fancy career, now she's got herself a rich husband who worships the ground she walks on. But she doesn't have any friends, does she.

MINDY.   Can't have everything.

GEORGEANNE.   This makes me feel so much better, I can't tell you. *(The phone begins to ring. As the other women watch, Meredith crosses to it, picks up the receiver and then puts it back down again. Pause.)*

TRISHA.   *(Looking out window.)* Well, finally, that bar looks like it's running smoothly, and I see a bottle of Beefeaters that has my name on it. Okay, ladies. Let's get this show on the road.

GEORGEANNE.   *(Groaning.)* Do we have to?

TRISHA.   It'll be fun.

GEORGEANNE.   Yeah, compared to a triple bypass.

TRISHA.   Don't even think about him, Georgeanne, he is scum.

GEORGEANNE.   He is. He is slime.

TRISHA.   He is garbage. *(Georgeanne winces.)* Oh, I'm sorry. I forgot.

GEORGEANNE.   I need about another bottle of champagne.

TRISHA.   Anyone care to join us?

MEREDITH.   In a minute.

TRISHA.   Mindy?

MINDY.   Why would I want to go out there? It's just the same old relatives who have been embarrassed by me my entire life.

TRISHA.   Okay, we'll see you two later.

GEORGEANNE.   Trisha, if I start acting like a real asshole, if you will just take me aside and smack me, I would greatly appreciate it.

TRISHA.   Babe, it's going to take everything I have to keep myself in check, so I'm afraid you are on your own.

GEORGEANNE.   God help us. *(They exit. Meredith stands look-*

29

ing out the window, an inscrutable expression on her face. Pause.)

MINDY. *(Her mouth full.)* Mm. You should try one of these little bacon wrap jobbies, Meredith, they are delicious.

MEREDITH. *(Not turning to her.)* No thanks, I'm not hungry. *(Pause.)*

MINDY. Well, now that Scott and Tracy are officially married, I guess that makes you and me sisters. *(Meredith turns and looks at her, blankly.)* I always wanted a sister.

MEREDITH. It's not all it's cracked up to be. *(She turns back towards the window. Pause.)*

MINDY. Are you glad to finally be done with school?

MEREDITH. Yeah, Mindy, I'm just thrilled to be back at home, living with my fascist parents.

MINDY. Well, have you thought about what you want to do?

MEREDITH. No.

MINDY. What is your degree in?

MEREDITH. English. It's completely worthless.

MINDY. No, it isn't. You can do a lot with that. You can teach, you can write copy, you can edit, you can go to law school —

MEREDITH. Oh, *yeah.* That's just what I want to do, become a hired gun for the ruling class. *(Pause.)*

MINDY. All I'm saying is you don't have to do what you studied for. My degree is in behavioral psychology, and I sell real estate. Which, I suppose, it's completely appropriate when you think about it. But you really should let me introduce you to some people I know, Meredith, I bet they could —

MEREDITH. I just want to move.

MINDY. Move into town? Well, shoot, I can help you find a great place, this is the perfect time to be looking, too —

MEREDITH. God, no. I want to get as far away from Knoxville as I possibly can. I hate this town, I hate everything about it. I want to go somewhere where I don't know a single person. Where nobody will bother me. Where people will just leave me alone. *(Pause.)*

MINDY. Well, I guess I'll go ... see if they have any of these meatballs left ...

MEREDITH. Uh-huh.

MINDY.   We'll see you down there.

MEREDITH.   Okay.

MINDY.   Bye-bye. *(She exits. Meredith stands at the window, watching something — or someone — below, a blank, impassive expression on her face. The phone begins to ring again, startling her. She does her best to ignore it, and after a moment, she begins to cry quietly, as lights fade.)*

ACT TWO

The scene is the same as before; it is a couple of hours later. From outside can be heard the sounds of the wedding reception in full swing: people talking and laughing, a band playing dance music, etc.

Trisha and Georgeanne are seated on either side of Frances, who sits in front of the vanity. They are performing a makeover on her. Trisha applies makeup; Georgeanne is preparing to apply nail polish. She has partially unfastened the back of her dress to get comfortable, revealing the back of an elaborate black lace bustier. Mindy is seated on the edge of the bed, holding a plate of food. Everyone except Frances has a cocktail. Most have removed their hats; they have all removed their shoes.

GEORGEANNE.   Okay, Frances, which do you want, Maple Melon Mist, or Cha Cha Chinaberry?
MINDY.   *(Her mouth full.)* How come makeup is always named after food?
GEORGEANNE.   What do you mean?
MINDY.   Well, like Cha Cha Chinaberry, Maple Melon Mist. Raspberry Whip. Tangerine Dream. Simply Strawberry —
TRISHA.   *(Picks up lipstick, reads label.)* She's right. Guess what this is called.
GEORGEANNE.   What color is it?
TRISHA.   Kind of an orangey pink.
GEORGEANNE.   Peaches and Cream.
MINDY.   Pumpkin Chiffon.
TRISHA.   Nope.
MINDY.   Wait, let me guess. Ah ... Nectarine Nights. No? Canteloupe! Canteloupe Cascade —
GEORGEANNE.   Kickass Carrot Cake.
TRISHA.   Nope.
MINDY.   Cha Cha Cheese Whiz!

GEORGEANNE.   Oh hell, what is it?

TRISHA.   Absolutely Apricot.

MINDY.   See? They *are* all named after food.

TRISHA.   Well, what else are they going to name it after, Mindy? What are they going to say, Bleeding Wound Red?

GEORGEANNE.   Did you decide which nail polish you wanted, Frances?

FRANCES.   Uhm, I'll take the red.

GEORGEANNE.   Good answer. Trisha, be sure and give her red lips, too.

TRISHA.   Well, now wait. Do you want to look fresh and natural, or do you want to look like a woman with a past?

FRANCES.   Oh, fresh and natural, I think.

TRISHA.   Hmm. I think we'll go for a more neutral lipstick color.

FRANCES.   I don't want to be too made up, now. I don't want him to think I look trashy.

TRISHA.   Don't you worry. When I get through with you, he won't stand a chance.

GEORGEANNE.   What's his name?

FRANCES.   Bradford.

GEORGEANNE.   Bradford what?

FRANCES.   He didn't tell me.

GEORGEANNE.   Bradford. Brad. Brad and Frances.

MINDY.   Only Brad I ever knew was my orthodontist. Brad Rosenblum. He had the hairiest hands. And he was always sticking them in my mouth.

GEORGEANNE.   Brad and Fran. Brad and Frannie.

FRANCES.   I hate being called that.

GEORGEANNE.   It's cute.

FRANCES.   It sounds too much like fanny.

TRISHA.   What does he do?

GEORGEANNE.   Trisha. He's a bartender.

FRANCES.   No, he's in law school.

GEORGEANNE.   Really?

FRANCES.   He only bartends part time, thank goodness.

TRISHA.   Well, you tell him he makes a superior martini.

GEORGEANNE.   Law school! Frances, you have scored. How

33

old is he?

FRANCES.   Thirty-six.

GEORGEANNE.   Thirty-six and he's never been married? That's not a good sign.

FRANCES.   He's been married once before. No kids, although he says he wants to.

TRISHA.   Divorced?

FRANCES.   No, she died.

GEORGEANNE.   Ugh.

TRISHA.   Poor thing.

FRANCES.   Four years ago.

GEORGEANNE.   Well, in a way, that's kind of — *attractive.* I mean, it makes him kind of tragic and mysterious.

FRANCES.   He feels like he's just now getting over it.

TRISHA.   Frances, your timing is impeccable.

MINDY.   I just had a horrible thought.

GEORGEANNE.   What?

MINDY.   What if he killed her?

TRISHA.   Mindy.

MINDY.   I'm serious. What if he goes around the country, marrying women and then killing them. Didn't you ever see that movie?

GEORGEANNE.   Yes! And you know what? He kind of looks like that guy.

MINDY.   Doesn't he?

GEORGEANNE.   He's got those shark eyes.

MINDY.   How did she die, Frances?

FRANCES.   He didn't say. *(Pause.)*

GEORGEANNE.   My cousin George works for the state patrol, I could get him to run a security check for you.

TRISHA.   I thought your cousin George was a nurse.

GEORGEANNE.   That's my other cousin George. I have three cousins named George, one named Georgette and one named Georgina. And my Aunt Georgia. We're all named after my grandfather.

MINDY.   What was his name?

GEORGEANNE.   *(Staring at her.)* George.

FRANCES.   Bradford is too nice to be a killer.

GEORGEANNE.   Uh-uh. Those are the ones you need to watch out for.

MINDY.   Wouldn't that be gross?

FRANCES.   What?

MINDY.   If you fell in a love with a real psycho killer? And you really loved him, and you married him and all, and then you found out what he was? What would you do? *(Pause.)*

GEORGEANNE.   Well, first thing, I would find a good support group for the wives of psycho killers, because I think I would need to talk to some people who really understood what I was going through.

MINDY.   Would you tell the police?

GEORGEANNE.   Come to think of it, I guess I would be kind of scared of him. *(Meredith enters, holding a cocktail. She locks the door behind her.)*

MEREDITH.   Y'all, I have got to get out of this dress. It is completely unnatural. Georgeanne, will you unzip me?

GEORGEANNE.   *(Doing so.)* What are you going to do?

MEREDITH.   I am going to be comfortable for the first time today, damn it. *(She maneuvers her way out of the dress, leaving it in a pile on the floor. Underneath she wears a strapless bra and a pair of boxer shorts. She is still wearing boy's athletic shoes.)*

TRISHA.   Meredith, you can't go out there and not be wearing that dress. You just can't.

MEREDITH.   Don't worry. I am not going out there again. It's a fucking zoo out there. *(She retrieves a T-shirt from the bathroom and puts it on, then begins to dig through a box of CDs.)* My crazy old Great Aunt Rosalie just came up to me and screamed in my ear, "Well! I guess we'll be seeing you get married next, honey!" You know what I said to her? I said, "Fat chance. You will be dead long before I am ready to put myself through this shit."

TRISHA.   You did not. *(Meredith puts a CD in the CD player.)*

MEREDITH.   Well, no, I didn't. But I had to bite my tongue to keep from doing it. God! I am so sick of listening to that cheesy band. *(Screaming, nihilistic rock & roll blasts over the speakers.)*

TRISHA.   What are you in such a bad mood about now?

MEREDITH. First Tracy yells at me because I took that thing off my head. "It's not optional," she says. "It's part of the uniform." Then Mama has to join in about how I have gotten too much sun on my shoulders and they're all freckled and just ruined. "It's not ladylike," she says, whispering to me like she was telling me I had B.O. Ladylike! Of course, to her, there are two types of women, debutantes and dykes, and guess which category I fall into. No offense, Mindy. Then poor Scott starts having a sneezing fit —

MINDY. He always does that when he gets nervous.

MEREDITH. — and the band is playing, "Tie a Yellow Ribbon." You know that hostage song? And all the old farts are dancing — Is there any of that joint left?

MINDY. Meredith, what *is* this music?

MEREDITH. You don't like it?

MINDY. It's really ... intense. Don't you have anything a little ... *less* intense?

MEREDITH. Sure, let me see if I can find something bland enough for you. (*She pulls the CD out and starts rummaging around.*) What are all y'all doing up here?

TRISHA. Frances has a date, and so we're giving her a makeover.

MEREDITH. A date? With who?

GEORGEANNE. Bradford the Bartender.

MINDY. And part-time psycho killer.

MEREDITH. What are you going to do?

FRANCES. Well, he said he knew of this place right outside town that was real pretty, and maybe we could just drive there and have some beers. (*The other women exchange looks.*) But then I told him I didn't drink beer, that I was a Christian, and he said, well shoot, we could go to McDonald's, that he just enjoyed talking to me. I thought that was real sweet.

TRISHA. That is.

FRANCES. He comes from a real small town too, we were talking about how scary a place like Knoxville can be. And he said as soon as he gets his degree he's going back to the country. Not to where he came, he doesn't think he can ever go back there, since his wife died —

MEREDITH.   She died?

MINDY.   Yes, and under very mysterious circumstances.

FRANCES.   He said he felt like he had to shut the door on that part of his life, and start all over with a clean slate. *(Mindy and Georgeanne trade looks.)*

GEORGEANNE.   Just like the guy in that movie.

MINDY.   Uh-oh. You better get him to show you some pictures of himself when he was younger, Frances. For all we know, he might not really be bald, he might have shaved his head to change his identity.

GEORGEANNE.   I bet Bradford is not even his real name.

MINDY.   You know what you do? Go to McDonald's with him, and then when he's not looking, you take something that he's touched, pick it up with a napkin, though, and just slip it in your purse, and then tomorrow you take it to the FBI.

GEORGEANNE.   If she's alive tomorrow.

MINDY.   Oh, I don't think he would kill her on the first date.

TRISHA.   *(Laughs.)* You two are horrible.

FRANCES.   He can't be a killer. He's a Christian. *(Pause.)* Of course, he's a different kind of Christian than I am, since he believes in drinking beers. I told him that was wrong and he said he didn't think so, but that he would be willing to talk about it. That's the main reason I decided to go out with him.

GEORGEANNE.   Really.

FRANCES.   A good Christian man is hard to find these days. There isn't a single one in my church group, except for the ones who are younger than me, but they don't count. I think the man should be older than the woman. *(Pause.)*

MINDY.   And taller, too, I bet.

FRANCES.   Well, sure. *(The other women avoid each other's eyes, trying not to laugh. Meredith has found the joint.)*

MEREDITH.   *(Holding up joint.)* Anybody want to smoke any pot?

TRISHA.   I'll take some.

MINDY.   I don't usually, but I think I'll make an exception today.

GEORGEANNE.   Oh, well, twist my arm. *(Sits next to Mindy on the bed.)* You are going to have to promise to keep me away from that food table, though. I dropped ten pounds for this wedding, I intend to keep it off for at least a week or two.

MEREDITH.   Ten pounds, how did you do it?

GEORGEANNE.   *(Dryly.)* I was motivated. *(As they pass the joint around, Frances coughs dramatically.)* Hey, how old were you when you first smoked pot?

MINDY.   Twenty-one. I was a late bloomer.

GEORGEANNE.   I was eighteen.

TRISHA.   Fifteen.

FRANCES.   I don't take drugs. I'm a Christian.

GEORGEANNE.   What about you, Meredith?

MEREDITH.   I was twelve.

GEORGEANNE.   Twelve!

MEREDITH.   You remember when I was in junior high, Trisha, you and Tracy let me spend the night at your apartment on campus? We drank black Russians and got high.

TRISHA.   Meredith, I am so sorry I corrupted you like that.

MEREDITH.   No, I loved it! I couldn't believe how cool you were. I thought you were *it.*

TRISHA.   Oh, hon. If you only knew how fucked up I was back then. *(Meredith puts a reggae CD on the stereo and begins dancing loosely; Mindy watches her.)*

MEREDITH.   So, Trisha, what's up with you and Tripp Davenport?

TRISHA.   Nothing.

MEREDITH.   Come on. I saw you talking to him for about an hour out there.

TRISHA.   Yeah?

MEREDITH.   You two seemed to really hit it off.

TRISHA.   I wouldn't know, I was on automatic pilot.

MEREDITH.   But you said he had that look.

TRISHA.   I'm sick of that look. It always leads to trouble.

GEORGEANNE.   I don't know, Trisha. He's pretty cute.

TRISHA.   Believe me, he's quite aware of that.

MEREDITH.   He's not *that* cute.

TRISHA.   He's pretty cute.

MEREDITH.   He's no Tommy Valentine.

TRISHA.   Thank God. I will say one thing about him, he has the best hands.

GEORGEANNE.   Hands?

TRISHA.   Yeah. You can tell a lot about a guy by his hands. They are just so amazingly beautiful. And also — oh, y'all are going to make fun of me.

GEORGEANNE.   No, we won't.

MEREDITH.   We promise.

TRISHA.   Well. It's not a man's feet. And it's not his shoes, either, you know those big black wingtip shoes like businessmen wear?

GEORGEANNE.   *(Not sure she wants to hear this.)* Yeah?

TRISHA.   It's a man's feet ... *in* those shoes. *(Pause.)*

MEREDITH.   That's really weird, Trisha.

MINDY.   My therapist would have a field day with that.

GEORGEANNE.   I like a good neck, myself.

MEREDITH.   Shoulders.

FRANCES.   Rear ends.

MINDY.   Well, personally, I prefer a nice set of hooters. *(Everyone laughs.)*

MEREDITH.   So, Trisha, do you like him or don't you?

GEORGEANNE.   She likes him a lot.

TRISHA.   How do you know?

GEORGEANNE.   Because I know you, Trisha, and I know how you get when you really like somebody. You light up like a goddamn Christmas tree and then you get all shy. And that is exactly what you have done today.

MEREDITH.   How old is he?

MINDY.   He's — *(Thinks.)* — twenty-nine.

GEORGEANNE.   Twenty-nine! Trisha, you old dog. *(Trisha looks at her.)* No, that's great. Go for the young meat.

TRISHA.   Georgeanne! That's only — three years younger than me.

GEORGEANNE.   Three strong, limber, and highly energetic years.

MEREDITH. What does he do?

TRISHA. I forgot to ask for his resume.

MINDY. He works for a bank, telling other people where to put their money.

GEORGEANNE. Way to go, Trisha, that means he's probably rich.

MEREDITH. Is he single?

MINDY. He just broke up with his girlfriend a couple of months ago.

GEORGEANNE. How do you know so much about him?

MINDY. He's my cousin, and he's the only one who never got weird when I came out, so I keep in touch.

GEORGEANNE. Is there anything wrong with him?

MINDY. No, he's a really nice guy.

GEORGEANNE. Damn. Trisha, you have the best luck of any woman I know.

TRISHA. I don't believe this. I have a simple conversation with him and now I'm supposed to be picking out my china pattern? What century are you women living in?

GEORGEANNE. Oh, right, I forgot. You're through with men.

TRISHA. No, I'm through with being disappointed. I have never met a man who could look at me and see anything but his own ego, and Tripp Davenport is no different. No offense to your cousin, Mindy, but I think I'll pass.

GEORGEANNE. He really got to you, didn't he?

TRISHA. I'm sick of it. I am. I quit. I'll just be an old maid. *(Pause.)*

FRANCES. Don't you want babies?

TRISHA. You don't need a man to have a baby.

MINDY. Well, actually you do, technically.

TRISHA. Yeah, but you don't have to cement yourself to him. Hell, he doesn't even have to know about it.

FRANCES. But that's so wrong.

MINDY. I don't think so. All the movie stars are doing it.

FRANCES. God wants you to be married if you have a baby.

TRISHA. How do *you* know what God wants?

FRANCES. Because the Bible says so.

TRISHA.   Frances, has it ever occurred to you that the Bible is a book that was written by men?

FRANCES.   The Bible is the holy word of God, Trisha.

TRISHA.   Well, I will grant you that it is the history of one culture's *quest* for God, but —

FRANCES.   *(Hotly.) That* is secular humanism talking, and *that* is the kind of talk that has got us into the mess we are in today, causing the collapse of family values and all decent morality. *That* is why there is so much crime and violence and licentiousness in this world, and that is why we are living in the end times and the rapture could happen at any minute. Any minute! *(Pause. Everyone is a little surprised by this outburst.)*

MEREDITH.   *(A laugh.)* Get serious.

FRANCES.   *(Upset.)* I *am* serious. Now, I will sit here and watch you all drink liquor and take drugs, every other word F this and GD that, honestly, you ought to be ashamed, you are *ladies.* But I will *not* tolerate you making fun of the Bible.

TRISHA.   Nobody's making fun of anything. Am I not allowed to have an opinion?

FRANCES.   Not if it is disrespectful to my religion, no ma'am, you are not. *(A pause.)*

TRISHA.   I'm afraid I have a little problem with that.

FRANCES.   This is America. I have a right to my beliefs.

TRISHA.   *(Evenly.)* Listen, Frances, I wholeheartedly support your right to live your life however you see fit. But you cannot exercise that right without extending the same courtesy to other people who might think differently than you do.

FRANCES.   My religion happens to be very important to me, and I don't want to listen to you criticize it.

TRISHA.   Then leave. *(Pause.)*

GEORGEANNE.   Trisha.

TRISHA.   I mean it. Go on, get out of here.

FRANCES.   *(Shocked.)* What?

TRISHA.   Go someplace where people don't have ideas. Where everybody is willing to trade their God-given intelligence for any old blind set of rules just because they don't want the responsibility of making their own decisions. I'm sure you won't have to go very far.

FRANCES. I —

TRISHA. But don't you *dare* tell me what I can and cannot talk about. You do *not* have the right to do that. *(A pause. Frances backs down completely.)*

FRANCES. *(Looking at her half made-up face in the mirror, weakly.)* But I can't go out there looking like *this.* I'm only half done! What would people think? *(She turns to Trisha, terrified. Tearfully.)* I don't look right!

TRISHA. Oh, good grief, Frances. Don't cry, your mascara will run.

FRANCES. I'm sorry.

TRISHA. Hon, I'm not mad at you, I just — oh, now look. Hm. Well, maybe we'll go for the woman with a past look instead of the fresh and natural, that way we can do a smudged charcoal thing around your eyes. Okay?

FRANCES. Thank you. I'm sorry. *(Trisha resumes the makeover on Frances. A pause, as the others exchange surreptitious glances. Georgeanne mounts stair-climbing machine.)*

MEREDITH. *(A stoned laugh.)* Look at my dress. Doesn't it look like a big old cake, just sitting there? My mother told me there is an art to wearing a gown, that I should just float down that aisle like a swan. I wanted to say, Mama, have you ever seen a swan walk? Anybody can float on a lake.

MINDY. She meant like this. *(Mindy puts down her plate, stands, and swoops across the room in a hyper, ultra-graceful manner.)*

GEORGEANNE. Hey, do that again.

MINDY. Okay. *(Mindy repeats the move. It is stunning and absurd.)*

GEORGEANNE. Where'd you learn how to do that?

MINDY. Miss Amelia's Charm School.

TRISHA. You're kidding. You went to charm school?

MINDY. My mother *made* me go when I was in sixth grade, I think she was dimly aware of my dyke potential and was hoping Miss Amelia would nip it in the bud.

GEORGEANNE. What else did she teach you?

MINDY. She taught us how to choose the right haircut for our face, and how to avoid shooting a beaver when we sat down. We had our own beauty pageant for graduation. The Princess Charming Pageant.

GEORGEANNE. Oh my God.

MEREDITH. That must have been so humiliating.

MINDY. Are you kidding? I loved it. I wore a nautical bathing suit with a little skirt attached, and high heels, and I played *Crimson and Clover* on my bassoon for the talent competition and I won.

GEORGEANNE. You did not.

MINDY. It was the high point of my life. I'm serious. It's been all downhill ever since.

GEORGEANNE. I would have thought you hated beauty pageants.

MINDY. Why? Because I'm a lesbian? Hell, no. I haven't missed a Miss America pageant in twenty years. Those girls are better than drag queens. Hell, they *are* drag queens. *(She performs another dramatic swoop and then stands on the bed.)* "I am just so thrilled to be poised on the brink of a fabulous career combining broadcast journalism and teaching handicapped children but most importantly being a good wife and mother and a good American. *(Turning.)* Here's my tits, here's my butt, here's my tits again. Thank you!" *(She waves insanely. The other women crack up laughing. Meredith gets up on the window seat and yells out the window to the guests below.)*

MEREDITH. Hey everybody! Here's my tits! *(Pulls down her bra and flashes her breasts, then waves insanely.)* Thank you! *(A shocked pause, then Georgeanne and Mindy cross to Meredith and pull her away from the window, as Trisha attempts to calm Frances, who appears to be hyperventilating.)*

TRISHA. Meredith.

MEREDITH. *(Laughing hysterically.)* I just flashed my *mother* —

MINDY. Meredith, you're drunk.

MEREDITH. Duh.

GEORGEANNE. Come on. You need to sit down. *(They seat her on the bed.)*

MEREDITH. I just flashed my mother. I couldn't help it. I saw her look up here with her face all pinched and I don't know, I just flashed my tits at her.

GEORGEANNE.   Did anybody else see you?

MEREDITH.   I don't know. Probably. I don't care. I'll just say that I didn't do it, and then she'll get confused. I'm sure she's heavily sedated by now, anyway. *(Suddenly serious.)* I'm glad I did it. It was fun.

GEORGEANNE.   There *is* a certain amount of freedom in letting your tits fly, isn't there?

MINDY.   I remember this one baby sitter me and Scott had, she would look at us real sweet and say "Do you all want to see my titties?" Well, of course we did. So we would sit there on the edge of my bed, and she would slowly pull up her blouse. And we would just look at them. *(She retrieves her plate and resumes eating.)*

GEORGEANNE.   How old was she?

MINDY.   Oh, I don't know, twelve, thirteen.

MEREDITH.   That's child abuse.

MINDY.   Please. A young girl who is proud of her new breasts is hardly child abuse. It was completely innocent.

GEORGEANNE.   Hey, I want to know something. Do you always eat like this?

MINDY.   Yes.

GEORGEANNE.   Then how the hell do you stay so skinny?

MINDY.   I'm extremely neurotic and high-strung.

GEORGEANNE.   You don't like pig out and barf, do you?

MINDY.   No. I just have a really high metabolism and burn everything off.

GEORGEANNE.   God. I hate your guts.

MINDY.   You do not. You love me.

GEORGEANNE.   In your dreams.

MINDY.   *(Mouth full of food.)* Kiss me.

GEORGEANNE.   Get away.

MINDY.   Kiss me.

GEORGEANNE.   *(Laughing.)* You are the grossest person alive.

MINDY.   Thank you.

GEORGEANNE.   Let me have some of that.

MINDY.   Oh please. Take it away from me.

GEORGEANNE.   I'm starting to miss those ten pounds I lost.

(Mindy hands Georgeanne her plate, then notices a demure little sundress in a floral print in Meredith's closet.)

MINDY. This is so cute. Meredith, is this yours?

MEREDITH. It used to be. Back when my biggest goal in life was to be in the junior league.

MINDY. I bet you looked real sweet in this.

MEREDITH. You would.

MINDY. What is that supposed to mean?

MEREDITH. Nothing. *(Pause.)* Just what I'd expect from a country club socialite like you.

MINDY. *(A laugh.)* I am hardly a socialite, Meredith.

MEREDITH. A little white girl dress like that.

MINDY. You know, that's about the third time I've heard you say something about white people. I hate to point this out to you, hon, but you aren't exactly Queen Latifah.

MEREDITH. Yeah, well at least I am not a hypocrite.

MINDY. Neither am I.

MEREDITH. So?

MINDY. *(Amused.)* You think just because you put a picture of Malcolm X up on your wall, that proves something? If you really cared about injustice as much as you let on, you'd be out doing something about it, instead of sitting up here with your portable CD player and your stairmaster and your five hundred dollar motorcycle jacket, complaining about how unfair things are. *(Meredith stares at her, then turns to Trisha.)*

MEREDITH. So, Trisha. Tripp Davenport looks like he —

TRISHA. Don't start. Okay, Frances, all done. *(She turns Frances around so she can look in the mirror.)*

FRANCES. Oh, my.

TRISHA. What do you think?

FRANCES. I never knew I could look like this! *(She turns to face the others. She looks quite glamorous.)*

GEORGEANNE. Frances, you look *hot.*

MEREDITH. Trisha! You should do this for a living.

MINDY. God. She looks fabulous.

FRANCES. I don't even look like myself.

GEORGEANNE. Trisha, where did you learn to do that?

TRISHA. *Years* of practice.

MINDY. Will you do me next?

TRISHA. Well —

MEREDITH. And then me?

TRISHA. I'll do one more and then I have to get back out there.

MINDY. Hot damn! *(She sits down in front of the mirror.)*

TRISHA. What do you want to look like?

MINDY. A truck stop whore. *(The telephone rings. Meredith answers it.)*

MEREDITH. What, Mother? *(Meredith suddenly erupts, and screams into the receiver.)* Bitch! Would you just shut up and leave me the fuck alone, for once? *(She slams the receiver down. The other women stare at Meredith, a bit taken aback. She looks at them, scowling, then suddenly bursts into laughter. Mimics.)* "Everybody could see your dinners, honey, plain as day." Dinners! That is totally Appalachian. *(The other women exchange looks. Meredith wanders over to the stair-climbing machine, mounts it and begins to tread lazily.)*

GEORGEANNE. That's what my mother calls them too.

MEREDITH. Those two are in rare form today.

GEORGEANNE. I can just hear them. "Kitty, I want to tell you, Tracy just looked radiant at her wedding. Just radiant. Why thank you, Eleanor, you know, Georgeanne looked radiant herself. Is she expecting another child? Heavens no, Kitty, Georgeanne just needs to lose about twenty pounds, she's a fat pig."

MINDY. You are not fat.

GEORGEANNE. Well, I certainly ain't skinny.

MINDY. I think you look fabulous.

GEORGEANNE. *(Unbelieving.)* Thanks.

MINDY. And I think it's high time women let themselves just be women for a change, and stopped trying to look like all these anorexic models that, face it, they look like men. Every time I turn on the TV, there's some high-attitude fashion bitch stomping around like she's such hot shit and I think, *this* is what I'm supposed to want to be? I would rather eat glass. *(To Trisha.)* No that's not right. I want something sluttier. Like dime store blue.

TRISHA.   Meredith, do you have any blue eye shadow?

MEREDITH.   I sincerely hope not. But check in that top drawer.

GEORGEANNE.   I don't think there's anything wrong with wanting to look *pretty* —

MINDY.   Good grief, neither do I. But these women who are willing to have their lips poofed up and their tits inflated and their ribs removed? I mean, come on. That sounds like a Nazi war experiment. Those ribs are there for a reason. And that fat sucking thing? I'm sorry. There is something desperately wrong with a culture which encourages people to go to such extremes. We think we are so civilized. But we're just as barbaric as those Aztec guys who played soccer with human heads. Look at this whole ritual today. Here's your sister in this white monstrosity, meant to symbolize that she is undamaged goods, it's like a sacrifice! And I mean, who in this day and age is a virgin when she gets married?

FRANCES.   *I* will be a virgin when *I* get married. *(Pause.)*

TRISHA.   Frances, really?

FRANCES.   Yes ma'am.

GEORGEANNE.   Get out of here.

FRANCES.   I am saving myself for the man that I get married to. *(Pause.)*

GEORGEANNE.   Frances. That is whacked. Because believe me, he ain't saving himself for you.

MINDY.   I think that's admirable. You hold out for Mr. Right, Frances.

TRISHA.   Hon, you are setting yourself up for a major letdown.

FRANCES.   What is wrong with wanting to be a virgin when you get married?

GEORGEANNE.   How old are you?

FRANCES.   Twenty-one.

TRISHA.   Haven't you ever been in love?

FRANCES.   Not that way.

TRISHA.   Haven't you ever had the hots for somebody?

FRANCES.   I have more respect for myself than that.

TRISHA.   Okay, forget about the sex. Don't you ever get

47

lonely?

FRANCES.   No. I don't, because I have Jesus in my heart. He is always there for me, ready to give me strength when I feel weak. To show me compassion when I feel anger. And to embrace me completely, in the deepest, purest love that there is. Whenever I need it. *(Pause.)*

GEORGEANNE.   I think I might like a date with Jesus.

FRANCES.   That's not funny.

GEORGEANNE.   I'm serious.

FRANCES.   Jesus didn't date.

GEORGEANNE.   Are you kidding? He was the biggest rock star of his day. I bet he had groupies coming out the wazoo.

MINDY.   I think it's rather interesting that he had twelve men in dresses follow him wherever he went.

FRANCES.   Those were *robes.* Jesus and his disciples did not wear dresses. *(Pause.)* Except on very formal occasions. *(She giggles briefly, then casts her eyes upward and mouths the word "Sorry.")*

TRISHA.   Meredith?

MEREDITH.   Uh-huh?

TRISHA.   Why do you have all these pictures of Tommy Valentine? *(Pause.)*

MEREDITH.   Where?

TRISHA.   Here, in this drawer.

MEREDITH.   Tracy must have left them there. This used to be her room, you know.

TRISHA.   Yeah, about ten years ago.

MEREDITH.   Well, I don't know how they got in there.

TRISHA.   Look at this one of him water-skiing. He must be all of nineteen.

GEORGEANNE.   *(Grabs photo and looks at it.)* Oh, would you just look at that stomach? God, how I hate him.

TRISHA.   He sure was beautiful, wasn't he?

GEORGEANNE.   Still is.

MINDY.   Let me see. *(Looks at photo.)* Yeah, he's okay. If you like that sort of thing. Wait a minute. This guy's here today.

GEORGEANNE.   Yep. He still is.

MINDY.   This guy made a pass at me.

GEORGEANNE.   What?

MINDY.   Yeah, I was standing around at the food table and he came up to me and said, we haven't met, but I feel like I know you. I said, you must be mistaken, because you do not know me. And he said, well, I would like to. How do I go about it? I just laughed and said, whoa, buddy, you are barking up the wrong tree.

TRISHA.   He is so shameless.

FRANCES.   That's the same thing he said to me.

GEORGEANNE.   What?

FRANCES.   Yeah, he remembered me from the first time I ever met him, up at Uncle Reece and Aunt Kitty's lake house? He said he always wished he'd gotten to know me better.

GEORGEANNE.   No.

FRANCES.   Uh-huh. He was real sweet. He suggested that we go out after the reception, but I told him I was already spoken for today.

GEORGEANNE.   That son of a bitch!

FRANCES.   I'm sure he just meant for us to, you know, talk.

GEORGEANNE.   Oh, I'm sure.

TRISHA.   Good grief. That boy should have the word "trouble" tattooed right across his forehead, just as a common courtesy. I mean, imagine. Here he is at his old girlfriend's wedding, and he has either slept with or made a pass at every one of her bridesmaids. Well, all except one. That is so incredibly rude.

GEORGEANNE.   Yeah, Meredith, you better be prepared for him to try to jump your bones next, you're the only one left. *(Pause.)*

TRISHA.   Oh, please. Don't tell me. *(Laughs.)* Somebody needs to put him on a leash. *(Pause. Meredith is silent.)* Meredith? What's wrong?

MEREDITH.   Nothing. *(She sits on the bed and starts to cry. A stunned moment, then they all gather around her.)*

TRISHA.   Honey, what is it? Are you okay?

MEREDITH.   I'm fine. I'm fine, I don't know why I'm crying, I'm so stupid.

TRISHA.   No, you're not stupid.

GEORGEANNE. Did he do something to you?

MEREDITH. No, he — I just — I had a — a thing with him, too. We had a thing.

GEORGEANNE. What?

MINDY. When?

MEREDITH. A long time ago. It was — it was okay, he didn't rape me or anything. Please don't ever tell anybody. Promise me you won't ever tell anybody. Especially Tracy.

TRISHA. I promise.

MEREDITH. We just ... we had a thing. Not for long. It's okay. It was okay.

MINDY. How old were you? *(Pause.)*

MEREDITH. I don't know. Twelve, thirteen. *(Pause. Georgeanne grabs her shoes and hat.)*

GEORGEANNE. That does it. I am going to find that sleazy fuckwad and tell him just what —

MEREDITH. Don't!

TRISHA. Georgeanne —

GEORGEANNE. He has it coming, Trisha!

MEREDITH. Don't! Please! *(Georgeanne exits.)* Trisha, don't let her!

TRISHA. Frances, you go after her, and do *not* let her make a scene.

FRANCES. But what can I do?

MINDY. Get that psycho killer boyfriend of yours to help. Go on. Stop her.

FRANCES. Okay. *(She finds her shoes and exits.)*

MEREDITH. She can't say anything to him, Trisha. She can't.

TRISHA. She won't, Meredith, they won't let her.

MEREDITH. I would die if anybody ever knew.

TRISHA. It's okay. You don't have to tell anybody.

MINDY. Yes, she does.

MEREDITH. He really liked me, Trisha. He really did. And now he won't even look at me. I went up to him outside, I was nervous as shit, and I said hey, Tommy. Remember me? And he said, "Well, sure I remember you. Hey there." But he wasn't looking me in the eye. And he *wouldn't.* He wouldn't

50

even *look* at me.

TRISHA.   Oh, hon. *(Pause.)*

MINDY.   What did he do to you, Meredith?

MEREDITH.   It's not like it sounds, he was really nice, he really — he really liked me. He did. He was always bringing me little presents whenever he came home with Tracy. Telling me how pretty I was getting to be. He came to my junior high swim meet when I won first place for the freestyle, it was one of the happiest days of my life.

TRISHA.   I remember that.

MINDY.   Tell me what he did. *(Pause.)*

MEREDITH.   He was here one Christmas, it was Christmas Eve, and everybody had gone to sleep. I was laying in bed. I was thinking about him. I was imagining what it would feel like. I had never even kissed a boy. *(Barely audible.)* And there was a knock on my door, real soft. It was like a dream. He said he thought it was time we got to know each other a little better. And Trisha, I wanted it. I wanted it to happen.

TRISHA.   That's only natural, Meredith. Everybody is curious about sex —

MEREDITH.   No, I wanted him. I wanted Tommy Valentine. I wanted him to fuck me.

TRISHA.   And there is nothing wrong with that. He is a good-looking, charming, sexy man. Of course you would want that. But there *is* something very wrong with him actually doing it. Very wrong with *him*.

MEREDITH.   I loved him.

MINDY.   That wasn't love, Meredith. That was abuse.

MEREDITH.   *(Angry.)* No it wasn't!

MINDY.   How long did it go on?

MEREDITH.   Just a few more times, then he said he thought we should quit, I mean, after all, he was engaged to my sister.

MINDY.   Listen to me. You need to talk to somebody about all this.

MEREDITH.   I can't tell —

MINDY.   I'm not talking about Tracy, or your parents. I'm talking about somebody who can help. What happened,

51

Meredith, was not harmless. It was abuse. You were sexually abused.

MEREDITH. *(Upset.)* Stop saying that.

MINDY. And it happens to a lot of women. You're not the only one. I know a lot of people it happened to. *(Meredith looks at her uneasily.)* You need to realize exactly what did happen, and how it affected you. And you need to be with people who have been through it. They can help.

MEREDITH. I could never tell anybody.

TRISHA. You told us.

MEREDITH. Yeah, and obviously that was a mistake.

MINDY. I have a number you can call, I'm going to give it you. I want you to promise —

MEREDITH. *(Angry.)* I'm okay.

MINDY. Just promise you'll think about it.

MEREDITH. It's not a big deal. God. You're trying to make it into this big thing, it *wasn't* —

MINDY. I'm going to leave it right here on your dresser, okay?

MEREDITH. Do whatever you want, I don't care.

MINDY. And I'm putting the names of a couple of people you can speak to directly on here, they're friends of mine, and they will —

MEREDITH. Look. Get this straight, Mindy. I am not interested in meeting any of your friends. I'm not.

MINDY. But they can help —

MEREDITH. Oh, I *bet.* *(Pause.)* What do you think, I'm an idiot, Mindy? I am not blind, I see the way you look at me. But I am not like you. I'm just *not*, okay? So it really wouldn't do much good for me to meet any of your friends. *(Pause.)*

MINDY. Meredith, I —

MEREDITH. What? Nobody asked you to butt into my life, did they? I don't recall anybody asking you to butt into my life. *(She removes her bathrobe, retrieves her dress from the floor and maneuvers herself into it.)* If you all will excuse me, I think I am needed outside. Trisha, can you zip me up?

TRISHA. *(Doing so.)* Are you okay, hon?

MEREDITH. *(Irritable.)* I'm fine. I wish everybody would stop acting like I was falling apart. I am not a child, you know! I am fine.

TRISHA. Well, I just want to tell you, if you ever need me, I'm here.

MEREDITH. Excuse me. *(She exits.)*

MINDY. Well, great. That's just great. Anything I can offer is going to get thrown back in my face as being some perverted seduction attempt. Meanwhile, a man can actually molest her while she's still a child and she calls it love. *(A burst of anger.)* That *fucking* son of a *bitch!* I swear to God, Trisha ... sometimes, I just can't believe how fucking ... how incredibly fucked up men are. They've fucked up the economy, they've fucked up the environment, and what the hell do they do about it? They fuck little girls! You don't mind if I rant, do you?

TRISHA. As long as you don't expect it to change anything.

MINDY. God knows, I don't want to be one of those dykes who hates men. I don't hate men, some of my best friends are men. I just hate them right now.

TRISHA. What on earth goes through a man's head while he fucks his fiancee's twelve-year-old sister? *(Pause.)* I wonder if it's too late for me to become a nun. I mean, I don't believe in God, and I've partaken of just about every sin there is, but I tell you what, that life is starting to look pretty good. *(Pause.)*

MINDY. I knew this day was doomed, from the moment when Scott first told me he was going to marry Tracy. *(Mockingly.)* Tracy, who requested that I not bring Deb who is my lover of *nine years* to the rehearsal dinner because they wanted to keep it just *family.* And I acquiesced because I didn't want another big scene, and now Deb is boycotting the wedding which *Tracy* has gone out of her way to let me know she is *very hurt* by. Bitch. *(Pause.)* She will never love my little brother the way he deserves to be loved. She will never *honor* him and *cherish* him, like she said she would today, in front of God and everybody. It just makes me so sad. And now here I am in this ridiculous dress, with a fucking pin cushion on my head, I look like a hooker from the Twilight Zone, and if I blow chunks, I'm going to be really upset. *(Georgeanne has entered during this tirade.)* I hate throwing up. You are totally alone when you throw up.

GEORGEANNE.   It's so humiliating.

TRISHA.   It's good for you.

GEORGEANNE.   Last time I threw up, I felt terrible, Chuck and I had been drinking tequila all night long in a totally misguided attempt to have *fun* together, and I just barfed all over the place, and felt so bad, and instead of trying to make me feel better, he just looked at it and said, "God, Georgeanne, I could reconstruct your entire meal. Don't you ever chew your food?" And then he poured a beer on my head.

MINDY.   I haven't thrown up in almost twenty years.

GEORGEANNE.   Twenty years? Really?

MINDY.   Really. Not since Scott became an Eagle Scout.

TRISHA.   Are you serious?

MINDY.   Yep. I'm too repressed.

TRISHA.   Oh, please. You're the least repressed person I've ever met.

GEORGEANNE.   You don't *not* throw up because you're *repressed.*

TRISHA.   You should throw up, Mindy, you really should. It's completely primal, you would feel so much better.

MINDY.   Maybe I will.

TRISHA.   You should throw up on Tommy Valentine.

MINDY.   *(With resolve.)* I will.

GEORGEANNE.   I got bad news for you guys. Tommy Valentine has already left.

TRISHA.   Oh, he's such a chickenshit.

GEORGEANNE.   No, I think he made a *friend.*

TRISHA.   You're kidding!

MINDY.   Why should that surprise you?

TRISHA.   Who?

GEORGEANNE.   Blonde hair, navy blue linen dress.

TRISHA.   The backless?

GEORGEANNE.   Yep. Who was that, do you know?

TRISHA.   Karen Murdoch. Tracy's boss at Pepsi.

GEORGEANNE. Well, *that's* perfect.

TRISHA. Now Tracy and Tommy can run into each other at business functions and be tense and peculiar together.

GEORGEANNE. Ten to one she has an affair with him now that she's married.

TRISHA. Who knows?

GEORGEANNE. Who cares? *(Pause.)*

TRISHA. *(To Georgeanne.)* So how are you doing, babe?

GEORGEANNE. Trisha, I am fabulous. I am so drunk I can barely walk. And I have my eyes set on a certain saxophone player who shall remain nameless. Mainly because I have no idea what his name is, nor do I want to know. I just want to get him drunk, have my way with him, and then leave him stranded on the side of the interstate without any pants. Naturally, he doesn't even know I'm alive.

TRISHA. His loss.

GEORGEANNE. Aw, that is so sweet, Trisha. *(She hugs Trisha warmly.)* Listen, I am really sorry for the way I just kind of blew you off after I got married. I did, didn't I?

TRISHA. Yeah, you did. But it's okay. You were so weird to be around, I was actually relieved.

GEORGEANNE. But I should have been there when you were going through all that with that lifeguard.

TRISHA. Don't worry about it.

GEORGEANNE. And as soon as I unload that deadbeat piece of wet toast that I married, and I think that may be real soon, I am going to have a lot more free time to spend with the people that I really care about like you.

TRISHA. You're on.

GEORGEANNE. I've missed you. *(She hugs Trisha again; she is getting sentimental.)*

TRISHA. Georgeanne, your dress is still undone.

GEORGEANNE. Oh, my lord. And I was just walking around outside with it like this! Well, hell, at least *somebody* got to see my new sixty-dollar bustier. *(She twists her body around in an attempt to refasten her dress, much to the amusement of Trisha and Mindy.)*

MINDY. You look like a dog trying to chase its own tail.

GEORGEANNE. Well, I can't help it, I am being held hostage by my underwear — *(She wobbles toward the window, with Mindy right behind her, still attempting to refasten her dress. Trisha already stands at the window, gazing out, searching. Teasing.)* Who are you looking for, Trisha?

TRISHA. I was trying to find Meredith —

GEORGEANNE. Yeah, right. *(Looking out.)* Look at Frances, stuck to the bar, drooling over Ted Bundy.

MINDY. Good grief. You straight women, throwing yourselves away on mass murderers and child molesters. It's such a waste. *(Tripp appears at the door. He is in his late twenties, charming, dressed in a tuxedo. He shouldn't be overly handsome, but definitely sexy. This man enjoys a good time.)*

TRIPP. Well, what the hell are you all doing up here? There's a party trying to happen outside.

GEORGEANNE. We were just trashing your sex, Tripp Davenport.

MINDY. I'm fixing to puke my guts out.

TRIPP. And I'm just in time.

GEORGEANNE. Some guys have all the luck.

TRIPP. *(To Trisha.)* Hi.

TRISHA. Hi.

TRIPP. I've been looking all over for you.

TRISHA. I can be hard to find, sometimes.

TRIPP. So I've noticed. *(Pause.)* Mind if I join you?

MINDY. No.

GEORGEANNE. Pull up a chair.

TRIPP. I have been cutting up the rug with your mother for the past half hour, Mindy. I had no idea she could dance like that.

MINDY. Are you kidding? She danced for the U.S.O. in Korea.

TRIPP. Get out of here. Aunt Betty?

MINDY. That's where she met Daddy. And that's where I was conceived out of wedlock and my entire dysfunctional family began.

GEORGEANNE. That is so romantic.

MINDY. She was nineteen years old. Barely.

TRIPP.   God. Isn't that weird to think about? When my dad was my age, he already had three kids.

GEORGEANNE.   I'll tell you what's really weird to think about. There are some things that we are already too old for. Some things that have just passed us by, that we will never get a chance for.

MINDY.   Like what?

GEORGEANNE.   Like I will never be a stewardess. *(Pause. Trisha laughs.)*

TRIPP.   You would have been a great stewardess.

GEORGEANNE.   I would have.

TRIPP.   What did you want to be when you were growing up?

MINDY.   I wanted to be a nurse.

GEORGEANNE.   You and my Cousin George.

MINDY.   A nurse! I am so sure. Can't you just see me giving some old coot a sponge bath?

GEORGEANNE.   I always wanted to be a teacher. Well, I wanted to be Miss Crenshaw, because her fiancé would come pick her up in a blue Chevy Malibu with a white vinyl top and he was so cute, he had a blond crewcut and his sideburns were darker than the rest.

TRIPP.   What about you, Trisha?

TRISHA.   I wanted to be that lady on *Mission: Impossible,* the one who had to pretend to be in love with dictators so she could double-cross them and then go back to her husband who always wore the mask so he could turn into that week's guest star? I thought that would be a great life.

MINDY.   *(To Tripp.)* What about you?

TRIPP.   Well, mine's kind of similar, actually. I wanted to be Ilya Kuryachin on *The Man from U.N.C.L.E.*

GEORGEANNE.   God, remember him? In fifth grade, every girl in my class was totally hot for him.

TRIPP.   And that's exactly why I wanted to be him.

GEORGEANNE.   I bet you wore a lot of turtlenecks.

TRIPP.   Would you all be totally grossed out if I took off my shoes?

MINDY.   I couldn't possibly be any sicker than I already am.

TRIPP. *(Untying his shoes.)* I have the hardest time with shoes, I've got this one pair of wingtips I wear to work, it took me forever to break them in but now they are the most comfortable shoes I own. I begged Scott just to let me wear them today because nobody would know, but you know what he did? He said he had to ask Tracy, and of course *she* said no, I had to wear the same stiff patent leather shoes as the rest of the ushers, and now my feet are about to kill me. *(Pause.)*

GEORGEANNE. *(Sneaking a glance at Trisha.)* Wingtips?

TRIPP. Yeah. *(Pause.)* What?

GEORGEANNE. Well, I guess I'll go see what's happening outside. Mindy, would you care to join me?

MINDY. No, but I will.

GEORGEANNE. I'm kind of hungry.

MINDY. Oh, please. Do not even mention food, or I will throw up on *you.*

GEORGEANNE. At this point, I probably wouldn't even notice.

MINDY. That makes you the perfect date. *(They exit.)*

TRIPP. Hi.

TRISHA. Hi.

TRIPP. How are you?

TRISHA. Well, it's been a day.

TRIPP. How so?

TRISHA. Oh, I don't know. This is a very weird wedding.

TRIPP. They always are.

TRISHA. They always start out fine, but everybody has such high expectations, and then gradually they just disintegrate, and things get ...

TRIPP. Hallucinatory.

TRISHA. Exactly. *(Pause.)* What about you?

TRIPP. What about me?

TRISHA. Are you having fun?

TRIPP. I always have fun.

TRISHA. Really?

TRIPP. Just about.

TRISHA. And why is that?

TRIPP.   I'm not sure. But I kind of like it that way, so I try not to question it too much.

TRISHA.   You're just an easy-going kind of guy, I guess.

TRIPP.   I guess.

TRISHA.   I would imagine you get into a lot of trouble that way.

TRIPP.   It's happened.

TRISHA.   And will happen again.

TRIPP.   We can hope.

TRISHA.   Why are we talking like this?

TRIPP.   Like what?

TRISHA.   Like a cheap version of Humphrey Bogart and Lauren Bacall in *The Big Sleep*.

TRIPP.   I don't know. Maybe we're possessed.

TRISHA.   I don't get possessed.

TRIPP.   Maybe we're nervous around each other.

TRISHA.   Why would we be nervous?

TRIPP.   Maybe we like each other.

TRISHA.   *Like* each other?

TRIPP.   Well, sure. What else are we going to do at this point?

TRISHA.   Liking each other just sounds so — I don't know, it sounds so innocent.

TRIPP.   Maybe it is.

TRISHA.   What are you going to do now, give me your I.D. bracelet?

TRIPP.   If you really liked me, you would carve my initials in your arm.

TRISHA.   What?

TRIPP.   My next door neighbor in seventh grade did that, so she would have a scar in the shape of her boyfriend's initials. I thought that was so — *ultimate*, to have a girl like you so much she would mutilate herself for you.

TRISHA.   I will never like you that much.

TRIPP.   Damn.

TRISHA.   A tattoo would be much easier.

TRIPP.   Don't get a tattoo.

TRISHA.   Why not?

TRIPP.   I hate tattoos on women.

TRISHA.   Oh, but you love them on men? Is there something you need to tell me, Tripp?

TRIPP.   You don't need a tattoo.

TRISHA.   Well, nobody *needs* a tattoo. People get them because they want them.

TRIPP.   I don't want you to have a tattoo.

TRISHA.   A minute ago we just liked each other, and already you're trying to run my life. This is a bad idea.

TRIPP.   So you're admitting that we do like each other.

TRISHA.   I'm saying we did a minute ago.

TRIPP.   At one point in time, we liked each other.

TRISHA.   I think we can agree on that.

TRIPP.   Good. *(Pause.)* Now what do we do?

TRISHA.   Who says we have to do anything?

TRIPP.   You know, you have this way of answering every question with a question —

TRISHA.   Do I?

TRIPP.   As if you have to challenge everything I say.

TRISHA.   Does that bother you?

TRIPP.   No, it doesn't bother me.

TRISHA.   Good.

TRIPP.   I like it. I need to be challenged. Sometimes I can be full of shit.

TRISHA.   No. I don't believe it. You?

TRIPP.   It's true.

TRISHA.   I'm shocked.

TRIPP.   It's hard to imagine you being shocked, somehow.

TRISHA.   Oh, I get shocked.

TRIPP.   By what?

TRISHA.   By how stupid people can be. How selfish. How people are so willing to add to other people's suffering.

TRIPP.   Wait a minute, are we going to have a real conversation, now?

TRISHA.   I don't know, what do you think?.

TRIPP.   I'm not opposed to it, I just need to shift gears a little bit.

TRISHA.   We don't have to, if you're not up to it.

TRIPP.   No, let's do it. Okay. Do you believe in God? Do you ever think about Death? When was the first time you had sex? When was the first time you really *liked* it? Do you ever feel guilty, just because your life isn't too terribly difficult?

TRISHA.   Never.

TRIPP.   Good, me neither. Let's go to the mall.

TRISHA.   The *mall?*

TRIPP.   Yeah. It's Saturday, we could go the mall, hang out with the teenagers at the multiplex, chow down on some Chick-fil-A? Shop for hours in the tape and record store without buying anything?

TRISHA.   We're not dressed for it.

TRIPP.   Why not?

TRISHA.   Oh, I couldn't.

TRIPP.   Trisha, this is uncharacteristically gutless of you, I'm surprised.

TRISHA.   I am thirty-four years old, I am not about to traipse around a mall looking like I just came from my prom. The only way I would do such a thing is with the assistance of major pharmaceuticals.

TRIPP.   Well, in that case. *(He produces a packet of cocaine from his pocket.)* Say hello to our surprise guest.

TRISHA.   *(Obviously pleased.)* No! I have a feeling you could be a bad influence on me.

TRIPP.   I have a feeling nobody is ever a bad influence on you.

TRISHA.   *(Suddenly serious.)* Tripp, I really like you.

TRIPP.   Oh, I bring out the drugs and suddenly I'm Mister Wonderful.

TRISHA.   You're not a coke head, are you?

TRIPP.   No, this is strictly a special occasion thing.

TRISHA.   Would you tell me if you were?

TRIPP.   Yes, I would tell you if I was. We don't have to do this.

TRISHA.   No, I want to.

TRIPP.   But now you're nervous, now you don't trust me.

TRISHA.   It's not that.

TRIPP.   What is it, then? *(Pause.)*

TRISHA.   I would really hate for you to be a coke head.

TRIPP.   Okay, let's make a deal. You don't get a tattoo, I won't be a coke head.

TRISHA.   Deal. *(Pause.)*

TRIPP.   We really don't have to do this.

TRISHA.   Well, what's the worst thing that could happen?

TRIPP.   We could talk a lot and be *really* interesting.

TRISHA.   We could have heart attacks.

TRIPP.   We don't have to do that much. I have kind of a low threshold, anyway.

TRISHA.   We could get arrested.

TRIPP.   We could spend the night in jail.

TRISHA.   We could just spend the night. *(Pause.)* Are you blushing?

TRIPP.   Well —

TRISHA.   You are, you're blushing.

TRIPP.   Maybe a little.

TRISHA.   Did I shock you?

TRIPP.   No, I just —

TRISHA.   *(Really enjoying this.)* Is that not the direction you were intending to go in?

TRIPP.   Well, of course it occurred to me, but ...

TRISHA.   You never expected me to *say* it. You thought it would just kind of happen.

TRIPP.   I guess. *(Pause, as they look at each other. Holding up cocaine.)* If we do, I don't think I want to do this.

TRISHA.   Why not?

TRIPP.   Because I think I'd like to have a clear head.

TRISHA.   We'll do it after.

TRIPP.   Oh, good, because I quit smoking.

TRISHA.   Okay, then. No sense hanging around here. Let's go. *(She grabs her purse and turns to him. A bit of a challenge. Pause.)*

TRIPP.   Wait a minute. I'm not so sure about this.

TRISHA.   Why not? *(Pause.)*

TRIPP.   I think I would like to get to know you better.

TRISHA.   Oh, brother.

TRIPP.   I'm not so sure I want to go to a motel, do drugs

and have sex, just for the hell of it, because I think there might be more to you and me than that.

TRISHA.   Do you think there's something wrong with going to a motel, doing drugs and having sex, just for the hell of it? Do you think that's bad?

TRIPP.   No, I don't.

TRISHA.   You're the one who pulled out the cocaine.

TRIPP.   You're right. And when I came to this wedding, that's exactly what I was looking for. But now that we're here, now that this is happening, I don't know.

TRISHA.   I knew it. Guys like you cannot deal with a woman who takes charge.

TRIPP.   Guys like me? I've been reduced to a *category*? Thanks.

TRISHA.   You don't want me to be the one who makes the move, do you.

TRIPP.   I don't want you to be an easy fuck in a cheap motel. For me, that usually works best when it's with somebody I don't really care one way or the other about.

TRISHA.   Why, Mr. Davenport. Are you saying you care for me? I'm touched.

TRIPP.   *(Frank.)* I'm saying there's something between the two of us that I don't run into every day. I felt it the first time I met you, and you did too.

TRISHA.   I don't think you have any idea what I feel.

TRIPP.   I think I do. I think it scares you, and I think that's why you left me in the middle of the reception and came up here to hide.

TRISHA.   I did *not* come up here to hide.

TRIPP.   Why else would you care if I was coke head?

TRISHA.   I *don't* care if you're a coke head, Tripp. I don't care if you're a liar, a thief, if you're married, I don't care if you're a child molester *and* a psycho killer and you're wanted in fifty states by the FBI! I just want to have a good time today. I *want* to go to a motel, do drugs and have sex, just for the hell of it. Okay? Forgive me for being so shallow. *(Pause.)*

TRIPP.   I don't buy that for a minute.

TRISHA.   I cannot believe how amazingly arrogant you are.

TRIPP. You can't believe somebody's calling your bluff.

TRISHA. Oh, fuck you.

TRIPP. Women like you —

TRISHA. Now *I'm* the category.

TRIPP. — you like to stay one step ahead, just out of reach, but you're always looking back to say, "Don't stop reaching."

TRISHA. Yeah, well, better one step ahead than one step behind.

TRIPP. You think that's where I want you to be? I just broke up with somebody who was perfectly happy to be one step behind me, I don't want that.

TRISHA. See? This is it. This is all about what *you* want. Well, I'm sorry, but I am not here to be who you want me to be. *(Pause.)*

TRIPP. All I know, Trisha, is that I've never met anyone quite like you before. I have fun when I'm with you, more fun than I've had in a long time. So I don't want to blow this chance to see what — to see where we could.... Okay, if you want to go to a motel, do drugs and have sex, fine. I just want you to know what I'm feeling before we do it, because it's not going to be insignificant. *(Pause.)* I don't want to be just another notch on your belt.

TRISHA. You don't want a lot of things, Tripp. Why don't you tell me what you *do* want?

TRIPP. I want you to promise me something.

TRISHA. Okay, here we go. What?

TRIPP. I want you to promise me that you won't leave your body after we make love. And that you won't completely write me off, because we did. *(Pause.)*

TRISHA. Well, since we're all being so wonderfully honest, thank you, I have to tell you, Tripp. I can't promise that. I know myself, and I know that's what I do sometimes.

TRIPP. I had a feeling.

TRISHA. I *will* promise to try not to let that happen.

TRIPP. And if you feel like it is happening, you'll tell me?

TRISHA. But you have to promise me something in return.

TRIPP. Fair enough.

TRISHA. You have to promise not to get all twitchy on me,

and start obsessing about me and turning me into something that I'm not.

TRIPP. I have to promise not to fall in love with you?

TRISHA. You have to promise not to get too intense too fast. I'm serious. You have to promise not to put any pressure on me. Because I have absolutely no patience for that.

TRIPP. I promise.

TRISHA. That was too easy.

TRIPP. I'll be as quiet as a church mouse, you won't even know I'm around.

TRISHA. I'll know. *(Pause.)*

TRIPP. So, we're agreed, here?

TRISHA. Uhm ... we *understand* each other.

TRIPP. Good. Let's go to the mall.

TRISHA. I am not going to the mall.

TRIPP. Well, where else can we go?

TRISHA. *(Exasperated.)* Where do you *live*, Tripp?

TRIPP. Actually, I live in Atlanta.

TRISHA. You don't live here in Knoxville? *(Pause.)* You don't live here in Knoxville? You just put me through all that and you don't even live in the same *town?*

TRIPP. I have a car.

TRISHA. *(Laughing in spite of herself.)* You are such an asshole.

TRIPP. Is this a problem, me not living here?

TRISHA. Actually, it makes you infinitely more attractive to me.

TRIPP. Well, that's a back-handed compliment. You really think I'd be so hard to deal with on a regular basis?

TRISHA. Probably. I am.

TRIPP. You can always come visit.

TRISHA. We'll see.

TRIPP. I'm a great cook. I make the best toast in three states.

TRISHA. I do need to ask you something.

TRIPP. What?

TRISHA. Are you averse to latex?

TRIPP. Not at all. I just bought a variety-pack. *(There is a commotion heard from below. They cross to the window and look out.)*

TRISHA.   Whoops. I guess I'm supposed to be out there.

TRIPP.   Oh, shit, I haven't missed that garter thing, have I? I love that, it's so stupid.

TRISHA.   Look at Georgeanne, waving her hands in the back like a wide receiver. She can't catch the bouquet, she's already married.

TRIPP.   Everybody else looks afraid of it. *(Pause. Cheers from below.)* Oh, her. Good.

TRISHA.   Frances. That's perfect.

TRIPP.   Are you sad because you didn't get it?

TRISHA.   Oh, right.

TRIPP.   Always a bridesmaid.

TRISHA.   Never a schmuck. So. Tripp. Where are you staying? With Scott's family?

TRIPP.   No way. I'm staying at a really nice hotel downtown.

TRISHA.   The Regency?

TRIPP.   No, the Quality Inn.

TRISHA.   Oh, yeah, that's a *real* nice place.

TRIPP.   You've been there?

TRISHA.   No, but I've always wanted to, I've heard such fine things about it.

TRIPP.   Well, perhaps you would allow me to be your escort.

TRISHA.   God. I've dreamed of this.

TRIPP.   We'll dine in the Lamplighter Room. Later, we'll take a moonlight stroll around the parking lot, before ducking inside Chuckie's Hideaway, where we'll sip Mai Tais and boogie to the disco beat of the Rhythm Rascals. Then we'll retire to my suite, order nachos and cheese whiz from room service, and watch *Pretty Woman* on HBO. How does that sound?

TRISHA.   Sounds suspiciously like going to a motel, doing drugs and having sex just for the hell of it.

TRIPP.   How can you take something so beautiful and turn it into something so sleazy and cheap?

TRISHA.   I am sorry. It sounds heavenly. I can't possibly imagine a more perfect evening.

TRIPP.   Tracy and Scott won't be having nearly as much fun.

66

TRISHA.   Really, they're going to be stuck in Jamaica. Look at her, she looks like a hot air balloon from this perspective, doesn't she?

TRIPP.   She sure knows how to work a crowd.

TRISHA.   Promise me something.

TRIPP.   Anything.

TRISHA.   If you ever see me dressed in something that ridiculous, please shoot me.

TRIPP.   Uhm ...

TRISHA.   If you really like me, you will promise.

TRIPP.   *(Surveying her dress.)* Trisha, if I make that promise, I'm going to have to shoot you right now. *(He turns her to him and puts his arms around her. They study each other for a moment, then she places her arms on his shoulders and they kiss.)*

TRISHA.   You are either a total con artist or the most naive man in America. Either way, I'm in trouble.

TRIPP.   That makes two of us. *(They kiss again. Suddenly, the door bursts open and in walk Georgeanne, Mindy, and Frances in quick succession, all holding champagne glasses, with Meredith lagging slightly behind. Georgeanne also carries several tiny tulle bags, filled with rice, tied with ribbons.)*

GEORGEANNE.   Hey. Quit it, you two.

MINDY.   Gross.

GEORGEANNE.   Trisha, we want to take a picture.

TRISHA.   Of what?

GEORGEANNE.   Of all of us. And we have to hurry, because I don't want to miss the chance to throw these bags of rice right at Tracy's head.

MINDY.   I'm going to throw some of those little cocktail weenies at her.

GEORGEANNE.   Everybody get on the bed. Meredith, go get that camera. *(Meredith goes into her closet.)*

TRISHA.   Frances, what is that you have in your hand?

FRANCES.   *(Beaming.)* I caught the bouquet!

TRISHA.   In your other hand.

FRANCES.   *(Sheepishly.)* Oh, that's champagne. I just wanted to taste it. I'm sorry.

TRISHA.   Hell, don't apologize. Here's to it. *(She raises her own glass in a toast; Frances does likewise.)*

FRANCES.   *(Glowing.)* To holy matrimony! *(Trisha stares at her.)*

TRISHA.   Can't we just drink to love?

MINDY.   Hear, hear.

FRANCES.   I'm sorry. To love.

GEORGEANNE.   Oh, please. You guys make me sick. *(Raises her own glass.)* To mindless sex in public places. Okay, Frances, you get down in front. And we'll be, like, your court. Meredith! I just had a great idea!

MEREDITH.   *(Comes out of closet holding Polaroid camera.)* What?

GEORGEANNE.   Do you know where Tracy's homecoming queen crown is?

MEREDITH.   Yeah, it's in here.

GEORGEANNE.   Get it!

MEREDITH.   *(Handing camera to Tripp.)* Here you go, Griffin Lyle Davenport the Third. You know how to use this?

TRIPP.   Isn't this the kind of camera that any idiot can use?

MEREDITH.   Uh-huh.

TRIPP.   Yeah, I know how to use it. *(Meredith goes back into the closet; Georgeanne steps back, directing everyone else.)*

GEORGEANNE.   Mindy, move a little to your left. Y'all leave a space for Meredith. *(Studies the tableau.)* We need sunglasses. *(Everyone goes for their purse.)*

FRANCES.   I don't have any.

GEORGEANNE.   Meredith! *(Meredith emerges from the closet holding a crown in front of her.)*

MEREDITH.   What?

GEORGEANNE.   *(Taking crown.)* Perfect. Do you have an extra pair of sunglasses?

MEREDITH.   I'm sure I do somewhere.

GEORGEANNE.   For Frances.

TRISHA.   Everybody still have their bouquets?

GEORGEANNE.   Here, Frances, let's get that hat off your head.

FRANCES.   Why?

GEORGEANNE.   Because you were born to wear a crown,

babe. *(She places the crown on Frances' head. Mindy arranges herself seductively, pulling the shoulders of her dress daringly low. Meredith finds a pair of sunglasses in one of her drawers.)*

MEREDITH.   What about these? They're kind of Jackie O.

GEORGEANNE.   Excellent. Oh, good, Mindy.

MINDY.   I want a cigarette.

MEREDITH.   *(Grabs her pack and offers her one.)* Here. *(Mindy looks at her, taking the cigarette tentatively.)*

MINDY.   Thanks.

MEREDITH.   *(Flatly.)* Sure. *(They are all on the bed now, decked out in sunglasses, arranged around Frances, who wears the crown.)* Wait, I want to wear my leather jacket.

GEORGEANNE.   I'm missing my bouquet!

MINDY.   *(Grabs Tripp's shoes off the floor.)* Hold these. *(Pause.)*

GEORGEANNE.   No, I think Trisha should hold these.

TRISHA.   Shut up.

MEREDITH.   Come on, Trisha.

TRISHA.   I hate you all. *(Trying not to laugh, she trades her bouquet for the shoes. Meredith, having donned her jacket, rejoins the others on the bed.)*

MINDY.   We. Look. Fabulous.

GEORGEANNE.   We *are* fabulous.

TRISHA.   Okay, Tripp. Tell us when.

FRANCES.   Oh, wait!

TRISHA.   What?

FRANCES.   I know I shouldn't, but ... Meredith, would it be okay if I wore your diamond bracelet?

MEREDITH.   Frances, I don't have a diamond bracelet.

FRANCES.   Well, I know I saw one. It's right over here — *(She crosses to the open jewelry box and retrieves the bracelet she tried on at the beginning of the play.)* If you say no, of course I will understand.

MEREDITH.   Frances. Those aren't diamonds.

FRANCES.   They're not?

MEREDITH.   No, who do you think I am, Liz Taylor? Those are dime-store rhinestones.

FRANCES.   Oh.

MEREDITH.   That whole thing cost me about six bucks. You

69

can have it.

FRANCES.   Oh, no, I couldn't.

MEREDITH.   Sure you can, it's my present, since you caught the bouquet.

FRANCES.   It's so *nice*, though.

MEREDITH.   It's junk.

FRANCES.   But —

TRISHA.   Frances, some things in life are gifts. You can accept them. You are allowed. *(Pause.)*

FRANCES.   Oh, my. Well, thank you so much.

MEREDITH.   You are so welcome.

GEORGEANNE.   Okay, Tripp. Tell us when.

TRIPP.   Everybody squeeze in. Good. This is some major babe action happening here.

MINDY.   Hell, yes.

TRIPP.   Now, when I count to three, say —

GEORGEANNE.   Cha Cha Cheese Whiz.

TRIPP.   One ...

FRANCES.   *(Beside herself.)* I feel so glamorous!

GEORGEANNE.   You *are* glamorous, damn it.

TRIPP.   Two ...

MINDY.   I just know I have something stuck in my teeth.

TRIPP.   Three — *(All the women shout "Cha Cha Cheese Whiz" as they are illuminated by the flash from the camera. Simultaneously, there is a general blackout except for a couple of specials, leaving the women momentarily in tableau, before the remaining lights fade.)*

PROPERTY LIST

ON SET

Vanity:

  Top: lamp

        wooden picture frame

        lotion bottle

        powder box

        Rachel Perry cosmetics bottle

        cold cream

        small yellow box with earrings

        "silver" brush and matching hand mirror

        rhinestone bracelet

        lighted standing mirror

        can of quick-dry nail polish

        small ceramic bud vase with cotton balls and
            emery boards

        tissue box

        small ceramic picture frame

        mirror tray

        2 bottles Sally Hanson nail polish

  Drawer, SR: "Jackie O." sunglasses

  Drawer, C: "Dime-store blue" eye shadow

              silver hand mirror

              14 snapshots of Tommy Valentine

              2 bars of soap

  Drawer, SL: black leather make-up bag

              triangular red leather make-up bag

  Garbage can, empty

Center seating area:

        Needlepoint rug

        2 chairs with heart-shaped pillows

        Table with:

            phone

            large brass ashtray

Window-seat area:

Ottoman

Stairmaster

Walkman strapped to SL handle of Stairmaster

Dumbbells tucked under SR pedal of Stairmaster

Small brass ashtray on window sill

End table under US window with: flowers

Window-seat:

Large square pillow

Small square pillow

2 bolsters

Bathroom:

Hamper with:

3 washcloths, folded, SR edge

flowered washcloth on top

large box of tissues on SL edge

Shelf:

2 bottles of nail polish (red, pink)

bottle of nail polish remover

tobacco "joint"

Bed area:

Bed with:

2 ruffled pillows upright against headboard

2 bolsters

3 pillows

4 stuffed animals

SL bed-side table with:

2 picture frames

lamp

SR bed-side table with:

lamp

Under bed:
    red crate with:
        clothes (on bottom)
        cardboard shoe box with jewelry box inside
        satin jacket
        green shirt
Bird cage

Stereo area:
    Top shelf with:
        doll
        2 candles
        3 picture frames
        "Fur is Dead" sticker
        sitting angel statuette
    Second shelf with:
        stereo unit
        amplifier
        CD player
        CD case for "Every Mother's Nightmare"
            on SR edge of stereo unit
        reclining angel statuette
        Dallas Cowboys hat
        2 fashion magazines
    cassette rack
    koala bear
    loosely stacked CDs and tapes
    2 ceramic vases with flowers
    satin box
    marble statue
    "Rats Have Rights" sticker

Chest of drawers, US wall:
    Top: tiara
             slippers

Crate with:
>CD of Peter Tosh
>small basket with roach clip

Crate with:
>books
>Polaroid camera with film
>sundress

Boy's shoes, loosely laced and tied

Closet:
>outside: rug
>inside: hanging shoe rack with shoes
>hanging clothes
>hanging wardrobe bag
>extra hangers
>on shelf:
>>box with sunglasses
>>6 shoe boxes
>>hat boxes
>>sweater

Entrance area:
>2 plant stands
>small table with: doily
>flower basket
>pillar, draped, with urn filled with flowers
>mirror
>2 candlesticks

PROP TABLE

Sunglasses (MEREDITH)
Bouquet with orange and white ribbons (MEREDITH)
Bouquet with orange ribbons (TRISHA)
Bag (TRISHA) with:

      condoms, in inside pocket, securely taped together, accordion folded

      black lighter, in inside pocket

      sunglasses, in main pouch

      yellow cosmetic bag, in main pouch, with cosmetics

      yellow lighter, in inside pocket

Bag (MINDY) with:

      ball point pen, retracted

      small billfold business cards, in outside pocket

      sunglasses

Champagne bottle (Don Perignon) (GEORGEANNE), 1/4 filled with bottled water

Backup champagne bottle (Piper Sonoma), 1/4 filled with water

Silver food tray (MINDY) with equal parts:

      cookies, crackers, celery sticks, carrot sticks, cantaloupe chunks, honeydew chunks, other fruits, cheese cubes, 1 falafel ball heated and cut into quarters, 2 chicken dogs heated and cut into quarters

SOUND EFFECTS

Telephone ring
Reception background noise:
    people talking and laughing
    band playing dance music

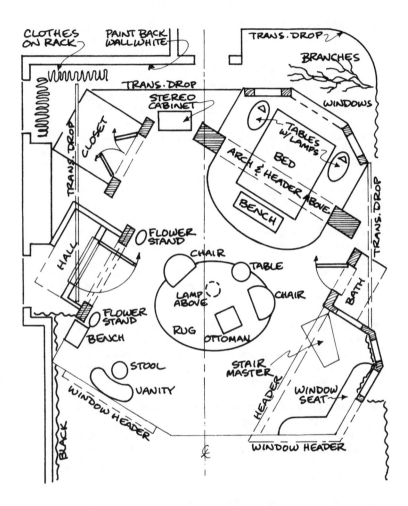

SCENE DESIGN
"FIVE WOMEN WEARING THE SAME DRESS"
DESIGNED BY
ROB ODORISIO
FOR MANHATTAN CLASS COMPANY

NEW PLAYS

★ **CLYBOURNE PARK by Bruce Norris.** WINNER OF THE 2011 PULITZER PRIZE AND 2012 TONY AWARD. Act One takes place in 1959 as community leaders try to stop the sale of a home to a black family. Act Two is set in the same house in the present day as the now predominantly African-American neighborhood battles to hold its ground. "Vital, sharp-witted and ferociously smart." *–NY Times.* "A theatrical treasure…Indisputably, uproariously funny." *–Entertainment Weekly.* [4M, 3W] ISBN: 978-0-8222-2697-0

★ **WATER BY THE SPOONFUL by Quiara Alegría Hudes.** WINNER OF THE 2012 PULITZER PRIZE. A Puerto Rican veteran is surrounded by the North Philadelphia demons he tried to escape in the service. "This is a very funny, warm, and yes uplifting play." *–Hartford Courant.* "The play is a combination poem, prayer and app on how to cope in an age of uncertainty, speed and chaos." *–Variety.* [4M, 3W] ISBN: 978-0-8222-2716-8

★ **RED by John Logan.** WINNER OF THE 2010 TONY AWARD. Mark Rothko has just landed the biggest commission in the history of modern art. But when his young assistant, Ken, gains the confidence to challenge him, Rothko faces the agonizing possibility that his crowning achievement could also become his undoing. "Intense and exciting." *–NY Times.* "Smart, eloquent entertainment." *–New Yorker.* [2M] ISBN: 978-0-8222-2483-9

★ **VENUS IN FUR by David Ives.** Thomas, a beleaguered playwright/director, is desperate to find an actress to play Vanda, the female lead in his adaptation of the classic sadomasochistic tale *Venus in Fur.* "Ninety minutes of good, kinky fun." *–NY Times.* "A fast-paced journey into one man's entrapment by a clever, vengeful female." *–Associated Press.* [1M, 1W] ISBN: 978-0-8222-2603-1

★ **OTHER DESERT CITIES by Jon Robin Baitz.** Brooke returns home to Palm Springs after a six-year absence and announces that she is about to publish a memoir dredging up a pivotal and tragic event in the family's history—a wound they don't want reopened. "Leaves you feeling both moved and gratifyingly sated." *–NY Times.* "A genuine pleasure." *–NY Post.* [2M, 3W] ISBN: 978-0-8222-2605-5

★ **TRIBES by Nina Raine.** Billy was born deaf into a hearing family and adapts brilliantly to his family's unconventional ways, but it's not until he meets Sylvia, a young woman on the brink of deafness, that he finally understands what it means to be understood. "A smart, lively play." *–NY Times.* "[A] bright and boldly provocative drama." *–Associated Press.* [3M, 2W] ISBN: 978-0-8222-2751-9

DRAMATISTS PLAY SERVICE, INC.
440 Park Avenue South, New York, NY 10016 212-683-8960 Fax 212-213-1539
postmaster@dramatists.com www.dramatists.com